THE CENTRAL ASIAN REPUBLICS

Fragments of Empire
Magnets of Wealth

Charles Undeland
and
Nicholas Platt

The Asia Society is a nonprofit, nonpartisan public education organization dedicated to increasing American understanding of the more than 30 countries broadly defined as the Asia-Pacific region. Through its programs in contemporary affairs, the fine and performing arts, and elementary and secondary education, the Society reaches audiences across the United States and works closely with colleagues in Asia.

Editor: Deborah Field Washburn
Editorial Assistant: Karen S. Fein
Editorial Intern: Mark Batistich
Designer: Susan Sokolski

Cover: Faience mosaic tile from the Gur-i-mir (Tomb of Tamerlane), Samarkand, Uzbekistan

Published by The Asia Society
725 Park Avenue
New York, New York 10021

All rights reserved. No part of this publication may be reproduced or transmitted in any form or by any means, electronic or mechanical, including photocopy, recording, or any information storage and retrieval system, without permission in writing from The Asia Society.

Copyright © 1994 by The Asia Society

ISBN: 0-87848-509-0

Printed and bound in the United States of America

♻ Printed on recycled paper

To Harold Newman

Contents

Map of Central Asia viii
Acknowledgments x
Preface xi
The Republics Today xiv

Introduction   1
The Myth of Central Asian Unity 1
National Identity and Politics 4
Economic Viability 10
Ethnic Populations of Central Asia 16

The Russian Presence in Central Asia   17
Aims 17
Deeds 21

Kazakhstan   29
Map 28
Politics 29
    President Nursultan Nazarbaev 29
    Clans 30
    Interethnic Relations and the Geographic Split 31
Economics 33
    Material Assets Profile 33
    Performance in 1993 34
    Non-CIS Involvement 35
Foreign Relations 36

The Kyrgyz Republic   41
Map 40
Politics 41
    President Askar Akaev 41
    Clans 43
    Interethnic Relations 44
Economics 47

 Material Assets Profile 47
 Performance in 1993 48
 Non-CIS Involvement 50
 Foreign Relations 50

Tajikistan   55

 Map 54
 Politics 55
  Clan Divisions 56
  Ethnic Divisions 57
  The Civil War 59
  The Opposition after the War 61
  The Current Government 62
  Foreign Involvement 64
  Post-War Tajikistan 67
 Economics 70
  Material Assets Profile 70
  Performance in 1993 71
  Non-CIS Involvement 72
 Foreign Relations 72

Turkmenistan   75

 Map 74
 Politics 75
  President Saparmurat Niyazov 75
  Political Opposition 77
  Interethnic Relations 78
  Islam 79
 Economics 79
  Material Assets Profile 79
  Performance in 1993 81
  Non-CIS Involvement 82
 Foreign Relations 82

Uzbekistan   87

 Map 86
 Politics 87
  President Islam Karimov 87
  Opposition Parties 89
  Clans 90
  Islam 91
  Interethnic Relations 93

The Fergana Valley 95
Economics 96
  Material Assets Profile 96
  Performance in 1993 97
  Non-CIS Involvement 99
  Foreign Relations 100

Foreign Influence in Central Asia 103

Turkey 104
Iran 108
Pakistan 111
China 113
The United States 117

Looking to the Future 121

A Note on Sources 127
A Note on Names and Spellings 129
Written Sources in English 131
Written Sources in Russian 133
Study Mission Agenda 135
Additional Sources 139
About the Authors 143

ADAPTED FROM
MAP NO. 3763 Rev. 1 UNITED NATIONS MARCH 1994

Acknowledgments

The authors wish to thank each of the host institutions and their facilitators for the visit: Vitaly Naumkin and Mavlon Makhkamov of the Russian Center of Strategic Research and International Studies in Moscow and Dushanbe; Bekhzod Alimjanov and Nadezhda Koblova at the National Association for International Cultural and Humanitarian Relations of the Republic of Uzbekistan in Samarkand, Bukhara, and Tashkent; Oumerseric Kasenov and Dastan Eleukenov of the Kazakhstan Institute for Strategic Studies under the President of the Republic of Kazakhstan in Almaty; and Esengul Beishembiev of the National Academy of Sciences of the Kyrgyz Republic in Bishkek.

Preface

Precious little was known about the five Central Asian countries of Kazakhstan, the Kyrgyz Republic, Tajikistan, Turkmenistan, and Uzbekistan when they emerged from the rubble of the Soviet Union in late 1991. But the sudden achievement of independence by these countries gave rise to great expectations. Many foreign analysts believed that the new states, linked by geography and Islam, could form a strategic belt to pose a counterweight to Russia, which was bound to reassert itself as the strongest power of the region.

Turkey's leaders were excited by the prospect of building a bloc stretching from China to the Mediterranean that was based on cultural and linguistic similarities and inspired by Ankara's brand of market reforms and secularism. Iran was expected to play on its proximity and cultural ties to the essentially Farsi-speaking Tajiks in the region. Pakistan hoped that it had gained a strategic, resource-rich Muslim "rear area" to support its confrontation with India.

Others saw great economic vistas opening up, with the Central Asian republics able for the first time to turn outward. Business people from Argentina to Japan saw a rich opportunity to exploit the area's vast natural wealth and starved consumer markets. Although the difficulties of operating in this underdeveloped part of the former Soviet Union became quickly apparent, the rush to the Central Asian El Dorado of gas, oil, and gold was on.

Two years later, we at The Asia Society decided it was time to assess developments in Central Asia firsthand. Beginning in October 1993, we obtained the services of a Moscow-based consultant, Charles Undeland. A fluent speaker of Russian and a determined, innovative traveler, he advanced and arranged a study mission for me to four of the five Central Asian republics in January 1994. The itinerary included a day of discussions on policy in Moscow, two days in Tajikistan, five days in Uzbekistan (with visits to

Samarkand, Bukhara, and Tashkent), two days in Kazakhstan, and a day in Kyrgyzstan. Undeland had visited Turkmenistan, the smallest in population and the most authoritarian of the republics. Given plane schedules, availability of fuel, and all the other imponderables, which would have added a week to our travel time, we decided to leave Turkmenistan out this trip.

The travel was challenging. Experts in Washington who knew the area looked at my itinerary and laughed. Aeroflot is unreliable at best. Gasoline and jet fuel are critically short, the hotels are abysmal, and some countries like Tajikistan are chronically short of food. Nevertheless, armed with jars of peanut butter, long underwear, warm boots, flashlights, and some U.S. dollars, we took off and succeeded in completing the trip on time, with only one difficult night spent trying to sleep in an Uzbekistan Airlines plane on the tarmac at Namangan en route to fogbound Almaty. We had dined on greasy cold chickens, pulled apart with bare hands and washed down with sweet Uzbek champagne, and a stale Snickers bar for dessert. But we got to Kazakhstan in time for my meeting with President Nazarbaev, which was what counted. In every country we had heavy schedules of meetings and conversations with political, economic, and cultural personages, some high level, many not. The net result was a much clearer picture of Central Asia.

If I had to give this trip a name, I would call it "The Ruined Empires Tour." We were traveling through the broken pieces of the Soviet imperial structure, pieces no longer able to relate effectively to a disconnected and confused center in Moscow, nor to each other. We were also seeing the spectacular shards of earlier empires in the region, those of Genghis Khan, Tamerlane, and the Bactrian successors of Alexander the Great, all jumbled together. The contrast between past and present is considerable. For all the region's historic ties to China, South Asia, and the Middle East, one is most struck by the huge Russian presence and the impact of 70 years of Soviet rule on the area's culture, politics, and economics. Even the physical environment has a heavy overlay of Soviet architectural grunge: Samarkand's fabulous mosques and *madrassas* (religious schools) are essentially isolated elements of a city whose residents live and work in concrete boxes built over the last 50 years. Indeed, the great bazaar towns in Pakistan—where the British built their new cities next to, rather than on top of, the ancient quarters—have far more of the atmosphere associated with the trading cities along the Silk Road than does post-Soviet Central Asia.

The study that follows is a combination of what we found out about contemporary Central Asia during our January 1994 visit and the research that Charles has conducted over the past half year. It is intended for those interested in the situation in Central Asia and the role other powers play on the ground. While describing the many common problems and features born of the republics' shared Soviet experience, the study focuses on the politics and economics of each republic in order to do justice to their complexities. At the end, after looking at all the pieces of the puzzle—the situation in each of the five countries and the role of foreign powers—we hazard some conclusions on directions Central Asia may take in the future.

In the years to come, The Asia Society plans to pursue its interests in cultural conservation, the visual and performing arts, and the needs of an expanding U.S. corporate community interested in Central Asia. We will hold lectures on the region and will provide platforms for distinguished speakers from the countries concerned. We also want to design ways to enable interested members to experience the rich historic sites that dot Central Asia. Whatever the challenges of travel, the ancient Silk Road cities of Samarkand, Bukhara, and Khiva are well worth the effort.

Nicholas Platt
President
The Asia Society

August 1994

The Republics Today

	Kazakhstan	The Kyrgyz Republic	Tajikistan	Turkmenistan	Uzbekistan
Size (in square miles)	1,049,150	76,621	55,251	188,455	172,741
Population	17,037,000	4,552,000	5,676,000	3,833,000	21,639,000
Capital	Almaty	Bishkek	Dushanbe	Ashgabat	Tashkent
President	Nursultan Nazarbaev	Askar Akaev		Saparmurat Niyazov	Islam Karimov
Chairman of the Supreme Soviet			Emomali Rakhmonov		

Introduction

THE MYTH OF CENTRAL ASIAN UNITY

Covering an area about twice the size of Mexico with slightly over 50 million people, the five Central Asian republics of Kazakhstan, the Kyrgyz Republic, Tajikistan, Turkmenistan, and Uzbekistan are commonly regarded as a homogenous unit. However, while the five countries share geography, many cultural traits, and the experience of Soviet rule, Central Asia is by no means a unified bloc. Over the course of its 3,000 years of recorded history, the area roughly spanned by the five modern republics was united under one state only for brief periods: first, when Genghis Khan swept through it in the thirteenth century, again when Timur (known in the West as Tamerlane) and his successors established an empire in the beginning of the fifteenth century, and finally as an appendage to Moscow from the second half of the nineteenth century until 1991. The five countries have different topographies, resource bases, ethnic relationships, political climates, and potential for development. They relate to each other no better than do the countries of Central America. Moscow's rule generated similar problems for each of the newly independent republics; more important, however, it created political and economic units that would be difficult to unite.

There are undoubtedly many cultural bonds among the indigenous peoples of the region, but also deep and important differences. One of the basic distinctions in the region is between the roughly 35-million-strong Turkic populations (Uzbeks, Kazakhs, Kyrgyz, Turkmens, and others) and the 4.5 million Tajiks, who speak an eastern dialect of Farsi (Persian). In addition, there are

9 million Russians and 30 smaller, locally important ethnic groups in the various republics. The second fundamental split in Central Asia is between the long-sedentary Tajiks and Uzbeks who populate the region's historic cities and the nomadic Kazakhs, Kyrgyz, Turkmens, and other peoples who began to settle only at the end of the nineteenth century and some of whom remain pastoral. The cultural differences between these two opposing ways of life left a deep imprint on the relationships among Central Asia's peoples. This divide remains in evidence today as Tajiks and especially Uzbeks dominate the region's bazaars and farms, while large numbers of Kazakhs, Kyrgyz, and Turkmens continue to herd animals.

Almost all of Central Asia's indigenous peoples are Sunni Muslim by heritage. Yet there are significant differences in the role of Islam in their cultures. Traditional Islam, with a clergy, is an important cultural factor among the Uzbeks and Tajiks. At the other end of the spectrum, Islam never had more than a superficial influence on the Kazakhs and Kyrgyz, in many ways simply being submerged into these peoples' traditional tribal beliefs. Islam was of greater importance to the Turkmen tribes, although their nomadic lifestyle precluded the development of a hierarchical clergy. The Communist regime diluted belief among all the peoples of Central Asia and compromised the official clergy. Yet Islam remained an important cultural force. With the fall of official atheism, Islam is reviving throughout Central Asia, especially in the cities and towns with high concentrations of Uzbeks and Tajiks.

Cultural closeness has more often led to friction than to friendship in Central Asia. Perhaps in part owing to the atmosphere of ethnic stereotyping prevalent throughout the old Soviet Union, the region's indigenous peoples frequently define themselves in contrast to their neighbors. Ethnic violence broke out in several instances in 1989 and 1990 and continues to lurk close to the surface, particularly where different populations share land or water.

Nonetheless, the idea of cultural similarities binding the republics remains attractive for many in these newly independent countries. Some intellectuals have promoted pan-Turkism, the notion that all Turkic peoples from China to the Mediterranean should unite on the basis of shared heritage, as a path for Central Asia's political development. However, the espousal of pan-Turkism remains more a philosophical exercise than a reflection of deep roots. As one self-proclaimed pan-Turkist confessed, even among likeminded Kazakhs, Uzbeks, and others divisions frequently overcome unity when it comes down to specifics. Furthermore, pan-Turkism fails to consider the place of Central Asia's non-Turkic peoples, mainly the Tajiks.

The governments of the five republics pay lip service to the idea of unity in the region based on common roots. Declarations abound on creating a "Union of Central Asian Peoples" and the like. In practice, however, politics among the countries has often been far from fraternal; republics have not hesitated to close off borders and fuel supplies when unhappy with their counterparts.

Central Asia is also home to wishful thinking about regional economic unity. With at least four of the five republics facing economic decline owing in part to the Soviet Union's dissolution, governments are grasping at any form of integration, be it under the Commonwealth of Independent States (CIS) or confined to Central Asia. These attempts at integration are more form than substance. The most concrete measure was the creation of a common market among Kazakhstan, the Kyrgyz Republic, and Uzbekistan in early 1994. However, thus far even that agreement has resulted only in the removal of already porous customs checkpoints.

A Central Asian trading bloc is more myth than reality and will continue to be so for the foreseeable future. With the exception of fuel and some agricultural products, there is little these countries want from each other. The crucial trade relationship for all the Central Asian countries is with Russia, although there has been a significant reduction in trade over the past two years. Furthermore, the Central Asian states find themselves competing over usage of the region's limited water supply as well as for foreign investment.

The lack of an economic fit also applies to the Economic Cooperation Organization (ECO), a trading bloc created by Turkey, Iran, and Pakistan, which Central Asia's republics joined, along with Afghanistan and Azerbaijan, in 1992. Although there are almost daily charter flights full of small-scale traders from Central Asia on shopping runs for consumer goods in Turkey and Pakistan, few big business deals are being cut. Central Asia's leadership recognizes that ECO is not going to provide the kind of capital or technology investment it desperately needs. In fact, as home to a rocket launch facility, the highest dam in the world, and other feats of Soviet engineering, Central Asia is more likely to transfer technology to other ECO nations. Governments in the region see ECO's value almost entirely as a transit route for their exports to the rest of the world.

Although not a bloc, the republics of Central Asia face many of the same problems, caused by shared geography and their relationship to the old "center," Russia. These common difficulties can be boiled down to the construction of a national identity and the development of economic viability, factors that will in large part determine the future of the Central Asian republics.

NATIONAL IDENTITY AND POLITICS

One of the many ironies of modern Central Asia is that, in a land that has been home to great civilizations for millennia, the current political entities have very little historical basis for their existence. The republics were carved out of previous Tsarist holdings by the Bolsheviks in the 1920s. Ostensibly following an official nationalities policy that accorded a territorial unit to each ethnic group, the Bolsheviks in fact were using a familiar imperial strategy of divide and rule by dispensing with the region's administrative units. Even with the best intentions, it would have been impossible to create homogenous republics because the ethnic groups were so interspersed. Inevitably, the new borders left some outside the republics named for them, creating fertile ground for territorial claims. This left fragile, artificial entities once the Russian "center" receded. Although the five republics have in all cases but one reconfirmed existing borders, there are grounds for disputing almost every boundary in post-Soviet Central Asia.

During the Soviet era, the borders meant little since they were purely administrative divisions of a single country. Instead of a sense of nationhood, a sense of loyalty to one's own locality and ethnic group developed. Even now, two-and-a-half years after independence, no one really thinks of himself or herself as an "Uzbekistani" or a "Tajikistani," whereas it does make sense to call oneself an Uzbek or a Tajik or a Tashkenti or a Leninabadi.

The emergence of these countries as sovereign states in 1991 was far from organic: few people, and certainly none in leadership, wanted complete independence from the USSR. Even local so-called nationalists pushed mainly for more cultural and economic autonomy, leaving the abstract goal of political independence for later. Four out of five leaders in Central Asia essentially endorsed the putsch launched by the Communist Party's old guard in August 1991. These leaders declared independence only when the collapse of the Soviet Union was a foregone conclusion. (In fact, many oppositionists in Central Asia claim that the republics' leaders declared independence in order to avoid undue questions from Moscow about their lack of support for Boris Yeltsin's stand against the coup's plotters.) Thus, political independence arrived suddenly and almost against the desires of the population. One Uzbek dissident has incisively noted that independence came too soon, preempting the development of a national political culture of Uzbekistan.

One of the strongest indications of these states' apathy toward sovereignty has been their reluctance to establish their own armed forces. The Central Asian republics took over Soviet units stationed on their territory only after Russia had stranded them in 1992, when it set up a separate defense ministry. Though in part owing to pragmatic recognition of the costs involved, the republics' stance contrasts sharply with that of the Baltic states or Ukraine, for which an independent army is an important symbol of sovereignty. Turkmenistan has pursued close bilateral military ties with Russia, while all other Central Asian countries have agreed to collective security agreements within the framework of the CIS, which Russia clearly dominates. Furthermore, each republic has devised a system of contracts to pay the mainly ethnic Russian officer corps it inherited.

Not surprisingly under these circumstances, political power in Central Asia's republics devolved, with slight variations, to the Communist-era administrative elite. The Kyrgyz Republic's president, Askar Akaev, is an exception: he was a career academic. However, he too has been compelled to join forces with the old administrative caste in order to stabilize politics in his country.

In understanding the region's political culture, however, it is crucial to avoid facile identification of these governments as "neo-communist." The fact that most of the leadership consists of former Communists in no way means that the governments are communist in ideology or that the old party structures have a stranglehold over politics. On the contrary, Central Asia's presidents perform the hajj to Mecca and espouse market enterprise with a vigor (though often not a substance) that would make Adam Smith proud. Of course, long years of tending the Soviet system left preconceptions about how to run the government and economy. Nonetheless, by the start of 1994 the leadership of every country in Central Asia had begun reforms, though in some cases modest ones, of the state-managed system. Furthermore, although the old Communist parties, now under new names except in Tajikistan, still are the dominant political movements in two of the five republics, they do not control government as they did under the USSR.

The driving issue in every republic is the power that Communist-era bosses wielded and now refuse to yield. Leaders in the region have demonstrated great flexibility in their positions in order to obtain short-term political security and gain. Except in Tajikistan, which suffered a debilitating and brutal civil war in 1992, each leader has established tremendous personal authority. In some cases these leaders have employed harsh measures to quash any challenges to their hold on power.

Again excepting Tajikistan, no indigenous force is capable of toppling the leadership any time soon. The lack of opposition is only partly due to government intimidation. The wave of political passions in the waning USSR, never very widespread, has been replaced by disillusionment with politics in general. Few people are ready to rock the boat for fear of repeating the experience of civil conflict in Tajikistan.

Furthermore, with independence, political activism has fallen to the conservative titular nationalities, most of which inhabit the countryside or smaller towns. Russians make up a large proportion of the urban populations (especially in the capitals); as a minority of former colonizers, Russians are not in a position to lead in shaping these countries' politics.

Finally, and most important, the tremendous, mainly adverse changes in the economy have shifted popular focus from government to the day-to-day problems of adapting to the new environment. By the same token, economic problems will spark any successful opposition. However, at least for the present, few believe that others would be able to do any better than the current set of leaders (who, after all, have experience as administrators) or that it is worth risking further economic dislocation by pushing for a change of government.

Central Asia's leaders exploit these sentiments, rationalizing that their concentration of power and sometimes harsh measures against opposition are necessary to ensure stability in countries without an established political system. Every leader except for Akaev stresses that his country is "not ready for full democracy" and that chaos will ensue without a strong leader. This hardly justifies the repressiveness of some of these governments, nor is it a long-term recipe for stability; however, these leaders are consciously trying to fill, at least in the political arena, the vacuum left after Moscow's abrupt departure.

Central Asia's leaders have also tried to build a sense of identity among their compatriots. The obvious starting point is ethnic affiliation, the ostensible basis for the creation of the republics in the first place. Governments have latched onto the revival of traditional culture, and the state actively sponsors national holidays, invariably including performances of traditional arts and games, to foster a sense of nationhood. Ethnic consciousness, rather than a sense of statehood based on political institutions, in all likelihood will continue to shape the development of a national identity. However, such emphasis on ethnicity is a double-edged sword. The majority of Central Asia's republics are home to significant ethnic minorities; therefore, governments must strike a balance between the cultural revival of the dominant ethnic group and reassurances to minorities of their importance to the country.

This is particularly important with regard to the key Russian minorities in each republic, for whom local traditional culture is the most foreign. A Russian minority uneasy about local ethnocentricity vastly complicates Central Asian governments' crucial relationships with Russia, and it endangers their mainly Russian-run industries. Thus, Central Asia's leaders have strenuously cultivated an image as champions of interethnic harmony while depicting (often inaccurately) their opponents as "nationalists" who will foment ethnic disturbances.

Emphasis on ethnic orgins rings a little hollow, since its advocates in government, like the urban elites in Central Asia from which they spring, are highly Russified. Under the Soviet Union, Russian supplanted the native language as the preferred means of communication among the Kazakh and Kyrgyz elite and, to a lesser degree, among the other indigenous peoples. Central Asians heavily competed for what was seen as the privilege of studying in Russia, and even today some among these elites deride their rural compatriots for speaking Russian with a poor accent. Three of the current leaders in Central Asia were educated in the European part of the Soviet Union, and two presidents even required tutoring in their "native" language in order to speak publicly. Furthermore, since the current leaders all rose to prominence by being loyal administrators for Moscow, they hardly fit the role of great ethnic leaders.

Central Asia's leaders must find a balance between their Communist backgrounds and the Islamic component to ethnic identity in the region. Central Asia's governments support the return to religion insofar as it is part of the traditional culture, but are deeply anxious about Islam's real and potential political dimension. For the very short term, however, the authorities in Central Asia have little to worry about. With some notable exceptions in Tajikistan and Uzbekistan, the politicization of Islam has been the exception and not the rule in Central Asia. Central Asia's governments have ruthlessly neutralized the political or even quasi-political manifestations of Islam or, in the case of Tajikistan, militarily defeated and expelled the Islamic elements of the opposition. Nonetheless, as an increasingly important societal force largely beyond the government's control, Islam will be a likely source of inspiration for movements that may threaten the former members of the Communist Party who now govern in Central Asia. Furthermore, current repression is apt to result in bitter backlash.

While ethnic identifications are likely to provide much of the glue needed to hold the new Central Asian states together, the other strong identification among the indigenous population—a fierce loyalty to region or tribe—has already proved a great obstacle to building national identity.

When the Bolsheviks recast the map of Central Asia, the local population, minus many of its old elite who had lost out to the Reds, was forced to adapt to the new political structures dictated by Moscow: the redrawn territorial divisions and the Communist Party. Since the party controlled everything but was hardly a meritocracy, contacts up the party ladder were crucial for success. A new system of patronage and support based on tribal and regional affiliations emerged in order to secure the perks and privileges the party could provide. In return for support on the way up, those who achieved power were obliged to take advantage of their position to help their own regional group.

This system is based on the power of the so-called clans (the term "clan" is frequently a misnomer, since many affiliations are essentially regional in nature with only weak blood connections). At the risk of great oversimplification, the Kazakh, Kyrgyz, and Turkmen clans are based mostly on blood ties, as these peoples settled comparatively recently and have retained many of their old tribal divisions. However, these clans also often contain a strong geographic link since they often settled together on traditional tribal lands. The historically more sedentary Uzbek and Tajik populations, on the other hand, are divided up into clans much more along the administrative borders imposed by the Bolsheviks in the 1920s (although family ties remain important because they determine who will dominate within the regional grouping).

Moscow allowed the clans to flourish in party structures as long as they remained absolutely loyal to the Soviet regime. In fact, the meshing of clan loyalties and Communist Party structures was a convenient way to deter local leaders from insubordination, since they all owed their livelihood to being in Moscow's good graces. As the final arbiter, Moscow was able to manipulate clan competition to keep its Central Asian possessions in line. In addition, Moscow always placed ethnic Russians in key posts in the republics (generally, the number two position in the Communist parties and the heads of key industrial enterprises).

Soviet-era politics led to intense jealousy and infighting among clans in each republic over the wealth controlled by the Communist Party. Furthermore, a perception took increasingly deep hold among Central Asia's populations that their interests were served only if their own clan was dominant in their republic's government. Now that Moscow no longer regulates politics, clan divisions are very dangerous. Tajikistan's brutal civil war was basically a struggle between clan alliances for control of the republic's central government. In other parts of Central Asia, national governments have succeeded, at least for now, in taking a variety of measures to temper clan rivalries. Yet the clash of clans over state appointments and contracts remains the most important political fault line in the new Central Asian republics.

ECONOMIC VIABILITY

Although some of the Central Asian states are rich in resources, they all face tremendous difficulties in creating viable national economies. Most of the problems can be attributed to the legacies of Soviet-planned economies, although other factors such as geography and resource bases also play a role. Even for oil-rich Kazakhstan and gas-rich Turkmenistan, overcoming the array of economic problems of the post-Soviet period will be a long and difficult undertaking.

Moscow dictated a division of labor under which the role of Central Asia's republics made sense only in conjunction with the contributions of the other 15 Soviet republics. With the exception of the ethnic-Russian-dominated capital cities and the northern and eastern parts of Kazakhstan, this role was principally as a source of raw materials for more industrialized parts of the Soviet Union. Under the byzantine logic of socialist integration, almost all manufactured goods and most consumer products were imported from Russia and elsewhere; thus Central Asia's economies are now scrambling to secure imports of consumer goods. The republics' limited industrial bases also rely on suppliers of component parts from and consumers of manufactured products in other republics, most often Russia. The dissolution of the Soviet Union wreaked havoc on these interdependent industries. The introduction of new currencies and the breakup of the united banking system hampered basic transactions. More important, newly sovereign countries embarked on uncoordinated and often chaotic price restructuring, which made it difficult for the various links in the Soviet chains of industrial production to stay in step.

Further complicating this problem is the fact that much of Central Asia's heavy industry, particularly in Kazakhstan and the Kyrgyz Republic, was devoted to Soviet military production. In addition to the general breakdown in trade, government contracts for military hardware have declined and the main contracting party (Moscow) is switching business away from local enterprises to Russian ones. In Kazakhstan alone, military-related contract volume fell by two-thirds in 1993 after a 50 percent drop in 1992; similar figures apply to the smaller defense-related industrial bases in other countries in the region. At the same time, Central Asia's republics neither can afford nor really want much of what their heavy industry produces. For instance, Kazakhstan possesses a plant that was a major producer of Soviet submarine torpedoes, a product not high on the essentially landlocked republic's wish list.

Socialist integration also created a jigsaw puzzle in the allocation of basic resources: every republic except for Turkmenistan is dependent on at least one other republic for fuel or electricity. In addition, the limited amount of water provided by the region's two main rivers, the Amu Darya and the Syr Darya, makes the downstream republics of Kazakhstan, Turkmenistan, and Uzbekistan dependent on the Kyrgyz Republic and Tajikistan. The chaotic and sometimes antagonistic nature of interrepublican relations after the Soviet Union's dissolution has frequently disrupted this delicate system of interlocking pipelines, electric cables, and rivers.

Not only do Central Asia's economies depend on the rest of the former Soviet Union and especially Russia to keep afloat, they also rely heavily on local ethnic Russian minorities for skilled labor to run their industries. A marked ethnic split exists among occupations in the Central Asian republics: the indigenous population dominates agriculture and light industry, while the Russians occupy heavy industry and high-technology service sectors such as communications. Many Russians argue that this is only natural, since they have a tradition of skilled industrial work which the indigenous populations lacks. Moreover, much of Central Asia's heavy industry consists of plants that relocated with their labor force from European areas of the Soviet Union during World War II. Moscow consciously maintained this dichotomy, making it notoriously difficult for the indigenous Central Asian populations to receive technical training in the Soviet Union. Economic reliance on ethnic Russians provides leverage in controlling the region.

It remains to be seen whether Russian technicians are going to stay to run the factories, pump the oil, and work the phones as the Central Asian states develop into independent entities. In large part this will depend on the relationship that Russia itself chooses to have with the region. Irreplaceable Russian skilled laborers are already emigrating in significant numbers, especially from the poorer states (Tajikistan and the Kyrgyz Republic). This emigration has contributed to the steep industrial decline felt all over the region except in Turkmenistan, where Russians are staying put. There are even reports of direct industrial loss owing to emigration: departing Russians have sometimes stripped equipment from the plants and taken it with them.

Parts of Central Asia face huge environmental damage caused by Moscow's policies. Relatively industrial Kazakhstan is particularly hard hit: in addition to its many noxious chemical and metal processing plants, this country is riddled with Soviet military test sites. Over 400 nuclear devices were detonated in Kazakhstan, including some surface blasts in the 1950s at the famous Soviet nuclear test site Semipalatinsk.

Soviet-style agriculture has also been harmful. Massive use of powerful pesticides and herbicides, some similar to Agent Orange, has literally poisoned the water table along the Syr Darya and the Amu Darya. Even worse, planners in Moscow vastly increased the number of canals drawing from these rivers in a drive to boost agricultural production. This effectively robbed the Aral Sea of the water it depends on from these two rivers. Once the fourth largest lake in the world in surface area (larger than all the Great Lakes except Lake Superior) and the sixth largest in volume, at current rates of decline the Aral will probably dry up entirely in the second quarter of the next century. The lake's diminishment is causing desiccation of a wide area surrounding its shores. Some scientists have asserted that the ultimate climactic impact of the disappearance of this body of water may be felt as far away as the Baltics. The effects of environmental degradation on the yields of downstream countries of Kazakhstan, Turkmenistan, and Uzbekistan are already being felt.

With the exception of cutting back on weapons testing, Central Asia's governments feel that they can do little to halt the environmental damage. Economics aside, the social consequences of shutting down the polluting factories or reducing cultivation to use less water are too great. In most cases, there is no alternative work for the potential unemployed. Moreover, closing industries might create ethnic tensions, since it would inevitably affect the Russian minorities disproportionately.

Even as they keep bloated industries and collective farms in operation, Central Asia's governments face a growing social and political challenge to create employment opportunities for their populations. High birth rates among the indigenous peoples, especially in rural areas, and improved health services have resulted in a population explosion; according to the 1989 census, Central Asia's five main indigenous ethnic groups more than doubled or even, in the case of the Tajiks, tripled their populations between 1959 and 1989. Unofficial unemployment has been rising steadily since the late 1980s as increasing numbers of students leave school and find few jobs available. There is significant migration from the overburdened countryside, dominated by stagnating state farms, to the cities, but urban centers themselves provide little work and even less housing. Ghettos of migrants looking for work have sprung up on the outskirts of the orderly, Soviet-built Central Asian capitals. All of these conditions have increased social tensions and contributed to rising crime rates.

As the least developed region in the former Soviet Union, Central Asia's republics suffer from weak infrastructure, although there are significant differences from republic to republic. Kazakhstan and Uzbekistan are the best served in terms of roads and railroads; with over 90 percent of their territory covered by mountains, the Kyrgyz Republic and Tajikistan are quite remote. Travel by air and land throughout the region is difficult owing to shortages of fuel and spare parts. Direct-dial international telephone lines are hard to obtain. Support services for foreign businesses remain primitive as the countries work toward establishing functioning service sectors.

Finally, Central Asia faces an economic challenge in its geography. This is the great irony of modern Central Asia: astride the historic Silk Road, the republics are at the periphery of global trade, having to rely entirely on other countries as conduits for their exports to most of the world. At present, this means working through Russian pipelines, roads, railroads, and ports. Although working with Russia does not have to be problematic, the uncertainties surrounding both the political relationship between the old center and the newly independent republics and the stability of Russia itself undermine the security of these transit routes. Central or regional Russian authorities or even local pipeline officials can put tremendous pressure on the Central Asian states if they so desire.

The alternatives to Russia are few and unattractive. The only rail link to a country other than Russia is with China's Xinjiang Uygur Autonomous Region to the east. However, this is not worth much since Xinjiang Region, one of the least developed areas of the country, is far from China's ports (though this alternative is still an improvement over the current route via the Trans-Siberian railroad). On the west, Central Asia borders the Caspian Sea, beyond which lies the volatile Caucasus region. Central Asia's southern neighbors are Iran and war-torn Afghanistan. Although only Afghanistan's thin Wakhan Corridor separates Pakistan from the region, this strip of land is extremely mountainous, and the equally rugged and underdeveloped Badakhshon region of Tajikistan lies on the other side.

Iran is logistically the easiest alternative to Russia as a conduit to the outside world. The two main export commodities from Central Asia at present—Kazakhstani oil and Turkmenistani natural gas—are located in areas relatively near the Iranian border. Furthermore, Central Asian states have a good working relationship with Iran, as the latter has placed a geopolitical interest in good relations with the region's governments ahead of exporting radical Islam. However, international ostracism of Iran limits the attractiveness of this route at present. Several officials in Central Asia have wryly noted that the greatest help that Western governments could provide the region would be to normalize relations with Iran.

INTRODUCTION

Central Asia's republics nonetheless are making efforts to wean themselves from dependency on Russia for contacts with the rest of the world. As Kazakhstan's President Nursultan Nazarbaev stated, "We have to seek new markets and we have to seek new routes to the wealth of the West."[1] Several flights from European and Asian cities now fly into the capitals of Kazakhstan, Turkmenistan, and Uzbekistan. Even Tajikistan has a weekly flight from London into its capital. There are plans to open an all-year highway that will run from Almaty, Kazakhstan, through Bishkek, the Kyrgyz Republic, to Kashgar, China, where it will join the Karakorum Highway leading to Pakistan. (This road, however, will be subject to frequent stoppages in the winter owing to heavy snowfalls in the passes in the Kyrgyz Republic and along the Karakorum Highway.) Turkmenistan and Iran have agreed to link their railroads by laying another 160 miles of track to connect their respective cities of Tajan and Mashhad. Turkmenistan has also signed memoranda with Turkey, Iran, Pakistan, and China on studying alternative pipeline routes. Tajikistan's government is planning to build a road from Dushanbe to Pakistan via Afghanistan. Central Asia's republics also hope that China will improve the links between its seacoast and Xinjiang Region.

All these initiatives notwithstanding, Central Asia's republics will rely heavily on Russia for the foreseeable future, at least until Iran's relations with the industrialized world improve. Even with an Iranian route open, Russia will remain a natural conduit from Central Asia to Europe and the Pacific via its port in Vladivostok. Russia's ongoing role as Central Asia's link to the outside world was underscored by a recent deal signed by Kazakhstan, Russia, and Chevron Oil to build a $1.4 billion pipeline from western Kazakhstan's oil fields to the Russian Black Sea port of Novorossiisk. However, continued wrangling with Moscow has brought negotiations over details of construction to a standstill, another indication of the problems the Central Asian republics face in working with Russia.

---

1. *Agence France Presse*, October 26, 1993.

Ethnic Populations of Central Asia
numbers of persons throughout the five republics

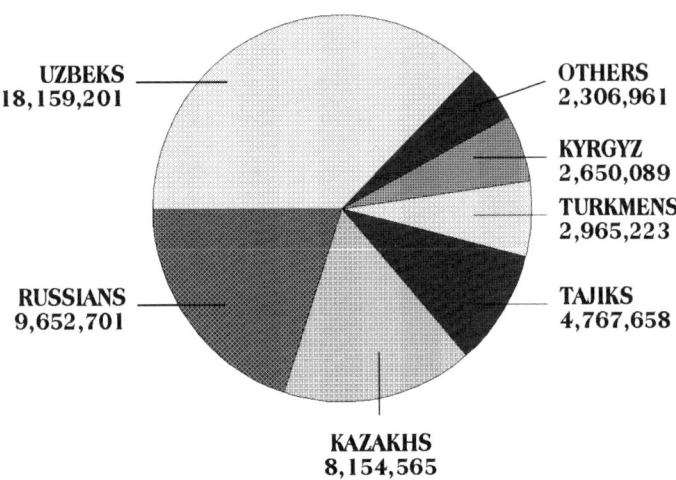

UZBEKS
18,159,201

OTHERS
2,306,961

KYRGYZ
2,650,089

TURKMENS
2,965,223

RUSSIANS
9,652,701

TAJIKS
4,767,658

KAZAKHS
8,154,565

The Russian Presence in Central Asia

Central Asia's questions of national identity and especially of economic viability all hinge to a large extent on what Russia and the 9 million ethnic Russians in Central Asia do. As officials in Central Asia often admit, many of the most important decisions affecting the region are still made in Moscow; the difference is that now local governments react whereas before they simply followed orders. However, these governments still have little room to maneuver, since it is economically and politically imperative for Central Asia's republics to retain close relations with the former Soviet center.

Russia is also in a chaotic process of defining its national identity. A key component of this search is coming to terms with its own borders and working out its relationship to its former possessions. While striving to undermine the Communist Party apparatus and General Secretary Mikhail Gorbachev, few if any in the present leadership in Moscow sought the dismemberment of the USSR. Furthermore, Russia's previous possessions are not geographically removed, making disengagement much more difficult than it was for other colonial powers.

AIMS

Since at least early 1993, politicians in Moscow, from generally liberal Foreign Minister Andrei Kozyrev to ultra-nationalist Vladimir Zhirinovsky, have shown unusual consensus in articulating a set of Russian goals in Central Asia and other parts of the former Soviet Union. These aims boil down to retaining political preeminence in the area; as one Kazakh scholar put it, "What is on the tongue of [Zhirinovsky] is on the mind of many Russian politicians and ideologues."[1] The objectives are as follows:

Protect the rights of ethnic Russians. President Yeltsin's government has long placed the treatment of Russians at the top of its agenda with other republics of the former Soviet Union; the nationalists' success in Russia's parliamentary elections on December 12, 1993, strengthened this stance. Aside from humanitarian concerns for its Russian brethren, Moscow admits that it wants to ensure that Russians abroad remain happy in order to preempt massive immigration, which cash- and housing-short Russia cannot handle. Keeping Russians abroad also serves as a valuable source of leverage in intergovernmental relations.

Maintain open and inexpensive access to strategic natural resources and facilities. Russia expects to have continued preferential access to these resources, many of which it would have a hard time replacing. Russia also wants to continue its use of important strategic facilities in Central Asia, most of which are in Kazakhstan. These facilities include nuclear and other weapons test sites in the Kazakhstani steppe and, above all, the Baikonur rocket launch facility.

Preserve markets. Many of Russia's manufactured goods find consumers only in Central Asia and other former Soviet republics, since they cannot compete on the international market.

Block the encroachment of other powers into the region. Russia considers Central Asia, like other former Soviet republics, to be its strategic backyard and is loath to allow other powers to gain a foothold in the area. Central Asian receptiveness to Turkish initiatives has drawn bitter responses and even threats from Moscow.

Block the advance of ideas or elements that would destabilize Central Asia and perhaps even Russia. These ideas and elements include political Islam, pan-Turkism, clan fighting from Afghanistan, and arms and narcotics smuggling from South Asia. Although most officials agree that none of these factors is at present a significant political force in Central Asia (though serious,

---

1. Oumerseric Kasenov, "Okazhet'sia li Tsentral'naia Aziia v vodovorote geopoliticheskikh igr? Razmyshleniia po povodu predlozhenii Rossiiskikh analitikov," *Aziia*, no. 1 (1994).

narcotics trading has not assumed political importance), Russia is worried about their potential growth. The success of such ideas would weaken Russian influence in the region and also might spread to Tatars and other peoples within the Russian Federation who have cultural backgrounds similar to those of the indigenous Central Asian populations.

Cut off effective subsidization of the region's economies. Except in the peculiar case of Tajikistan, Moscow wants to shed the burden of supporting Central Asia's economies. Under the Soviet Union, the Central Asian republics received the highest amount of transfers from the all-Union budget; transfers accounted for up to 45 percent of the republics' budgets. Moscow believes that the soft credits it has issued to the region since the USSR's breakup effectively continue this practice, though these credits have most commonly been to purchase goods in Russia.

The hegemonic nature of Russia's aims reflects a mind-set in the country's political elite that does not see the other republics of the former Soviet Union as sovereign entities in international relations. According to this train of thought, Russia has a special role in the region. Russian politicians express bitter incomprehension when accused of neoimperialism; Moscow feels that it is doing the world a favor by maintaining stability in these fragile former Soviet republics.[2]

These sentiments are especially strong with regard to Kazakhstan, the country with which Russia shares its only border with Central Asia: a 4,000-mile boundary drawn without any topographical basis across the Eurasian interior. Russians do not commonly consider Kazakhstan to be part of Central Asia; the term for Central Asia used most frequently in Russian denotes only the Kyrgyz Republic, Tajikistan, Turkmenistan, and Uzbekistan. While many Russians are ready to shed what they see as a culturally distinct, poorer Central Asia, few will consider letting

---

2. See Fiona Hill and Pamela Jewett, "'Back in the USSR': Russia's Intervention in the Internal Affairs of the Former Soviet Republics and the Implications for United States Policy Toward Russia," Report of the Strengthening Democratic Institutions Project, John F. Kennedy School of Government, Harvard University (January 1994); Suzanne Crow, "Russia Asserts Its Strategic Agenda," *RFE/RL Report*, Vol. 2, no. 50 (December 17, 1993).

go of Kazakhstan, particularly its ethnic-Russian-dominated northern and eastern parts. Russian claims to at least a part of Kazakhstan's territory were most poignantly expressed by the famous and widely respected Russian author Alexander Solzhenitsyn, who in 1991 called for the creation of a Slavic state composed of Belarus, Russia, Ukraine, and northern and eastern Kazakhstan out of the carcass of the USSR.

Russia seeks to hold Central Asia in its political embrace and as a source of raw materials while keeping the poorer regions at arm's length economically. Some Russian analysts describe this stance as a kind of "Monroevsky Doctrine" across the former Soviet Union, which can easily be attained by clever use of Russia's presence in the region.[3] However, the contradiction between political domination and economic disengagement has bedeviled the formulation of a consistent policy in the region.

The chaos of politics in Moscow also hampers the development of a clearcut Russian stance in Central Asia. Neither Russian President Yeltsin nor Prime Minister Viktor Chernomyrdin pays much attention to crafting relationships with the other republics of the former Soviet Union. Both make general assertions of Russia's prerogatives, leaving their ministers to do the talking on specific issues. The lack of direction at the top is complemented by a lack of coordination among various government agencies that handle relations with the area. The Foreign Ministry, Defense Ministry, Finance Ministry, and Economics Ministry often have conflicting agendas, largely along the fault line between geopolitical and economic objectives. Although Deputy Prime Minister Alexander Shokhin officially carries the portfolio of CIS relations, he has concentrated on economic issues (he is also economics minister) and left key areas such as collective security or rights of Russians to other officials.

Finally, the ostensible structure for coordinating relations between Russia and Central Asia in the post-Soviet era is the ineffectual CIS. In its two years of existence, the CIS has produced a large paper trail of agreements that have been at best spottily implemented. Although Russia and the Central Asian states (with the

---

3. See, for instance, Andranik Migranian, "Rossiya i blizhnie zarubezhie," *Nezavisimaya Gazeta*, January 5, 1994.

exception of Turkmenistan) have been among the strongest promoters of the commonwealth, all sides have shown few qualms about flouting CIS obligations when it suited their interests. Russia sees the CIS—an organization it clearly dominates—as a tool that facilitates continued Russian presence in the region. At the same time, Russia has irritated Central Asia in key instances by ignoring the bloc's guidelines on coordinating economic policy.

DEEDS

There have been four major issues in Russia's relations with Central Asia since the breakup of the Soviet Union: intervention in Tajikistan, economic disengagement and the fate of the rouble zone, exploitation of control over pipelines to pressure Central Asian governments, and pressure over ethnic Russians' rights. In the first two cases, Russia's leaders have demonstrated a lack of coherent policy unnecessarily damaging to Russia's relations with Central Asia. In the last two cases, Moscow acted with greater purpose but employed tactics that greatly soured relations with countries in the region.

Intervention in civil-war-riven Tajikistan is motivated by Russia's geopolitical aims. After it lost 25 soldiers in an attack by the Tajik opposition in July 1993, Russia bluntly outlined its justification for its actions: to ensure the safety of the remaining ethnic Russians (estimates of whom vary from 80,000 to 150,000); to maintain the border of the CIS (which Russia openly considers to be its own) from infiltration of arms and narcotics from Afghanistan; and, most important, to ensure that no outside influences, such as radical Islam or even ethnic Tajiks in Afghanistan, gain the upper hand anywhere in the CIS. Russia has made it clear that it considers Tajikistan to be its exclusive sphere of influence.

Yet Russia's actions in securing its sphere of influence have been inconsistent. During Tajikistan's civil war, Russia's 201st Motorized Infantry Division stationed in the republic provided arms to both sides, defended installations for the opposition, and then stood aside to let the forces behind the current government seize power. Since the war's end in December 1992, Russia's Defense Ministry has focused on strengthening the border with Afghanistan, thus essentially fighting on the side of the current government. Beginning in the summer of 1993, Russia's Foreign Ministry called for stabilizing measures in Tajikistan proper, including negotiations with the opposition to reduce tensions along the frontier. Meanwhile, in bowing to the geopolitical aims of shoring up a pro-Russian government, Shokhin signed off on agreements providing Tajikistan with numerous credits and allowed the republic to stay in the rouble zone.

For almost a year Moscow was unable, unwilling, or both, to force a government in Dushanbe that is totally reliant on Russian financial assistance to sit down at the negotiating table. Some argue that Moscow was being disingenuous in dealing with the opposition and that a Russian military establishment bent on continuing the Afghanistan war is really determining policy. However, successful negotiations would serve Russian interests by halting the opposition's attacks on Russian soldiers and contributing to the stabilization of Tajikistan. Moreover, talks finally are under way, owing in part to Russian pressure. This suggests that Russia's inaction was the result of uncertainty and lack of attention in Moscow—at least in the Foreign Ministry—rather than clever subterfuge.

Geopolitics took a back seat to Russia's financial difficulties during negotiations on maintaining a common rouble zone with Central Asia's two largest republics, Kazakhstan and Uzbekistan (the Kyrgyz Republic and Turkmenistan had earlier decided to introduce their own currency). Throughout 1993, Russia's economic reformers led by Finance Minister Boris Fyodorov worked to shore up the rouble's value by cutting back on credits to other CIS states. Their efforts were greatly helped when Russia's Central Bank suddenly, in violation of CIS agreements on advance warning to other states in the event of currency changes, removed all old Soviet roubles issued between 1961 and 1992 from circulation, leaving only new, 1993-issue banknotes. Several republics, including Kazakhstan and Uzbekistan, were left with only old roubles in circulation; Moscow was happy to continue fulfilling their currency needs with its own now-useless old roubles. The two Central Asian republics naturally became dumping grounds for all of Russia's unconverted Soviet roubles.

Russia then agreed in principle to create a new rouble zone, but shortly thereafter set conditions that would force Kazakhstan and Uzbekistan to bail out. Moscow demanded that the other republics improve their own economies, achieving a level of government deficit and inflation similar to Russia's, in order to receive new, 1993-issue roubles. Since the Soviet rouble was a lame duck, Russia suggested that Uzbekistan, Kazakhstan, and others introduce interim currencies while they improved their economies. Otherwise, Russia was prepared to provide 1993-issue roubles in the form of an intergovernmental loan if the republics provided a large amount of collateral in gold and hard currency, agreed to strict guidelines over fiscal policies, and accepted an exchange rate for old to new roubles of three to one. After abruptly dumping its old roubles on much smaller Kazakhstan and Uzbekistan (the only other countries using the rouble at that point were impoverished Armenia and Tajikistan), Russia justified its rigid conditions on the grounds that it was worried about an undue increase in its money supply should these republics introduce their own currencies after receiving allotments of 1993 roubles. Kazakhstan and Uzbekistan balked at these conditions, hastily introducing their own currencies on November 15, 1993.

After this, Moscow did another about-face and agreed to keep Tajikistan—whose economy lags farthest behind Russia's in every parameter—in the 1993-issue rouble zone, providing it with the necessary banknotes in January 1994.

While cutting Kazakhstan and Uzbekistan adrift is a logical step to enable Moscow to get a handle on its own currency, it deals a strong blow to Russia's geopolitical presence in the area and also may create an economic loss in the long term. Russia lost an important lever over the other republics when it forced them out of the rouble zone. And although they do not question Russia's right to have its own exclusive currency, Presidents Nazarbaev and Karimov are angry about the way this was achieved and the impact of Russia's actions on their countries.

Amazingly, Russian officials continue to speak of eventual reintegration when the republics' economies become as strong as Russia's, although why the republics would willingly seek to return to Moscow's fold once they could stand on their own economically remains unexplained. Moscow has vigorously discouraged the broadening of economic ties, sternly warning the Central Asian nations that they would have to choose between

Russia and the CIS on the one hand, and economic association with their southern neighbors on the other. Yet Shokhin himself noted, "Since these states didn't receive the desired support through the common rouble zone...[they] will, of course, try to reorient their economies toward Turkey, China, [and] Iran, and sell their strategic resources at a higher price."[4] Russia's economic retreat may in the long run reduce its access to Central Asia's raw materials, since these countries will seek alternative economic ties.

Russia has taken advantage of its monopoly over pipelines carrying Turkmenistani gas and Kazakhstani oil to the West to put pressure on the two Central Asian republics to accept greater Russian access to their mineral wealth. Although Turkmenistan had shown a desire for good relations with Russia in any case, Moscow reportedly decided to turn the screws on the small desert republic by withholding $185 million in earnings from natural gas sales to Europe at the end of 1993. This may have been a decisive factor behind the especially pro-Russian stance, replete with assurances of Russia's place in the development of the republic's gas industry, that Turkmenistan's President Niyazov adopted in December 1993.

Russia has reduced the amount of oil it is willing to transport from Kazakhstan's Tengiz field to less than half of what flowed when the old Soviet state oil concern was pumping. Russia has also laid down a series of costly and apparently unnecessary conditions to obstruct the building of a new pipeline. The price for Moscow's cooperation is clear: Russian officials have called for an equity share in Kazakhstan's landmark $20 billion deal with Chevron to develop Tengiz. With Russia allowing only one-fifth the amount of oil that Chevron had projected to be exporting as of early 1994, the company has been forced to cut back on development until an agreement can be reached with Russian authorities. It appears that Russia will have its way. Other Western oil and gas companies in the republic are taking note and figuring out how large a cut they will need to give Russia in order to secure their own deals.

No issue has irritated the leadership in Central Asia more than Moscow's persistent pressure for ethnic Russians' rights. For their part, Russians abroad air three general ethnically related complaints: preference is given to the titular nationality group in gov-

---

4. *Moskovskie novosti*, November 21, 1993.

ernment appointments; Russian is no longer the state language and is being phased out of administration; and educational opportunities and professional prospects appear to be shrinking as the titular nationalities increasingly dominate the republics. Local leaders believe these complaints are exaggerated, claiming that their governments' measures simply rectify the privileges granted to Russians when Moscow ruled.

Some of Central Asia's leaders are suspicious that Moscow's concern over Russians is a pretext for undermining their own local control. Given Russia's other aims in the area, there is cause for wariness. Russia's main policy thrust since the second half of 1993 has been to put pressure on the Central Asian states to accept dual citizenship. Aside from reassuring Russians who were suddenly cut off from the "center" after the Soviet Union's dissolution, Moscow argues that dual citizenship would give it the necessary legal basis to intervene on behalf of the Russians abroad. At the same time, there is potential for serious infringement of the Central Asian states' sovereignty—especially in the eyes of these countries' leaders, who deny that discrimination exists. In late November 1993, President Nazarbaev bluntly aired his concerns: "Whenever one starts talking about the protection of Russians in Kazakhstan, not Russia, I recall Hitler, who began to 'support' the Sudeten Germans at one time."[5]

Moreover, Russia's vigor in pushing dual citizenship has not been matched by attention to other problems faced by Russians in Central Asia. Moscow's squeeze on credits to other republics and its destruction of the rouble zone hit industry in Central Asia—the labor force for which is overwhelmingly ethnic Russian—harder than other sectors. Russians in Kazakhstan and Uzbekistan expressed a feeling of abandonment when Moscow's conditions torpedoed the rouble zone.

Moscow's pressure on the issue has produced some results: Turkmenistan agreed to dual citizenship; President Akaev of the Kyrgyz Republic supports the idea, although he can do little to implement it as dual citizenship is forbidden by Kyrgyz law; Tajikistan's government is thinking of making Russian a second state

---

5. *Interfax*, November 24, 1993, cited in Fiona Hill and Pamela Jewett, "'Back in the USSR.'"

language; and Uzbekistan and Kazakhstan recently agreed to a series of measures designed to shore up cultural and economic ties between ethnic Russians and their historic homeland (although nothing approaching dual citizenship). Correspondingly, confrontational rhetoric over the issue has waned since the beginning of 1994.

Central Asian governments largely accept Russia's regional preeminence, rejecting only perceived attempts to subvert their control over their states' internal affairs. In many ways, Central Asia's goals invert Russia's: the region's republics would like maximum economic cooperation while keeping Russia at arm's length politically. Nonetheless, facing significant internal divisions and other regional players including nuclear China, religious Pakistan, feuding Afghanistan, and radical Iran, Central Asia's stability-conscious governments continue to prefer—at least publicly—the devil they know in Russia. Between the end of December 1993 and March 1994, four of the five Central Asian leaders met with Yeltsin, seemingly in an effort to outdo one another in demonstrating their strategic closeness to Russia and readiness to address Russia's concerns in the area, specifically on the issue of protecting ethnic Russians.

The emerging character of the relationship between Russia and Central Asia's republics is one in which deep links force both sides to pursue close ties that, in turn, constantly suffer from Moscow's erratic vision of post-Union relations. As the economically and strategically dominant power, Russia is the protagonist vis-à-vis a mostly reactive Central Asia. Thus, relations for the near future will be determined in large part by the level of consistency in Russia's own policy. This depends on Moscow's ability to sort out its geopolitical and economic objectives, coordinate the management of relations among Russian government agencies, and neutralize the issue of ethnic Russians' rights.

The most important question over the long term will be the extent to which changes in the economic, cultural, and military ties between the Central Asian states and Russia affect their willingness to accept Moscow's political domination of the region. While for at least the next few years the Central Asian states have little choice but to play Russia's game in order to retain vital ties, their ability to develop alternatives will inevitably encourage a more independent stand.

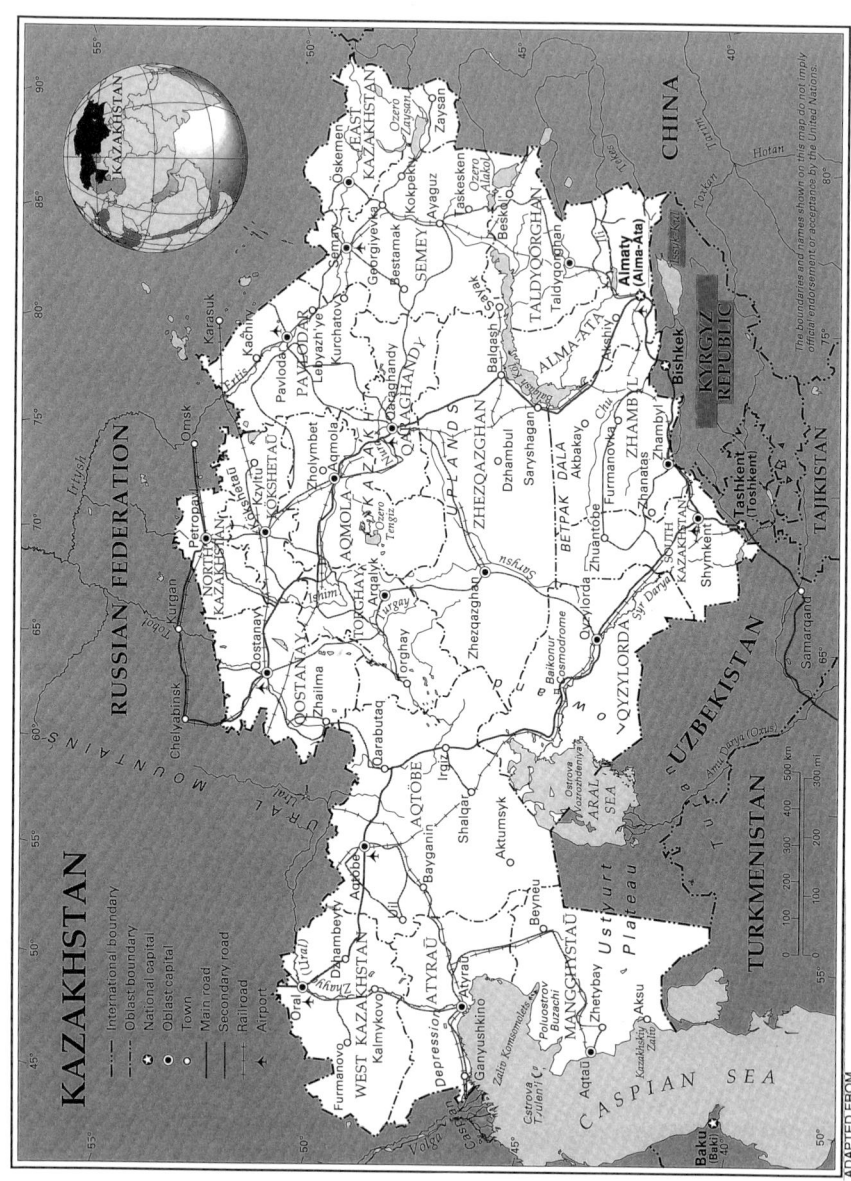

KAZAKHSTAN

POLITICS

President Nursultan Nazarbaev

Kazakhstan enjoys a high degree of stability relative to other countries in the CIS undergoing a similar period of social change and difficult economic reforms. Much of this stability stems from President Nursultan Nazarbaev's firm and basically unchallenged control over domestic politics. Nazarbaev's success is doubly impressive given the almost equal numbers of ethnic Kazakhs and Russians in the population and the existence of political movements based on ethnicity. Indeed, the Nazarbaev government commonly uses the specter of civil or ethnic violence in other CIS states, most notably Tajikistan to the south, both to discourage political opposition and to justify putting it down.

Nazarbaev's political career began in the mid-1970s in the *Komsomol* (Young Communist League) and then the Communist Party. He rose rapidly through the party ranks, reaching the position of first secretary in 1989. When Kazakhstan became independent in 1991, Nazarbaev had the loyalty of most government workers, since virtually all of them had been members of the party. The Communist-era elite continues to make up most of the government cadres; however, Nazarbaev has not simply converted the old Communist Party apparatus into his own "presidential" party. He studiously avoids party affiliation, although he clearly favors and receives support from the Union of Popular Unity of Kazakhstan, the leadership of which is drawn heavily from officials in the president's office. The old Communist Party was renamed the Socialist Party in late 1991 and has adopted a quasi-oppositional stance.

Nazarbaev has shaped the state apparatus to minimize any rival source of power. Under the constitution adopted in 1993, the prime minister and the cabinet are directly accountable to him. The president appoints governors of all the country's oblasts (regions) and has the power to remove people unsatisfactory to him. Information-gathering centers in each oblast provide a steady flow of data to the president's office in Almaty.

Nazarbaev has earned genuine popular support for his role in maintaining ethnic harmony in the face of displeasure on the part of some Kazakh nationalists and Russians deprived of their former privileged status, and for his efforts to salvage many of the economic benefits of integration among the republics of the former Soviet Union.

Despite its popularity, the Nazarbaev government has taken few chances. Although several independent political movements exist, the government has refused to register parties with purely ethnic Kazakh or Russian agendas, citing the need for stability. Nazarbaev's government reportedly made it very difficult for candidates critical of the government to register and campaign for the parliamentary elections on March 7, 1994. At the same time, the government put forward a "presidential list" of candidates, which received heavy state support. The media remains under the government's close watch, with some newspapers shut down for their critical stance. On the whole, however, Kazakhstan's record on civil liberties is good by Central Asian standards.

Clans

Ethnic Kazakhs are historically divided into three clans or *zhuzes* (the Kazakh for "one hundred," recalling a military nomadic grouping of horsemen). The senior *zhuz*, in the south, is the most numerous and powerful; the middle *zhuz*, in the north, is the most loosely knit, having been largely diluted by the massive Russian presence in the area; and the junior *zhuz*, in the west, is the smallest and most closely knit. The large Russian minority in Kazakhstan (which comprises 37 percent of the population) has made it impossible for the *zhuzes* to wield the influence on the republic's politics that clans do in other Central Asian countries. In addition, the pressures put on the Kazakh people by the Soviet regime, including unparalleled physical decimation and the forcible assimilation of numerous outsiders (Russians, Ukrainians, Volga Germans, and Koreans) weakened clan ties.

Members of the senior *zhuz* dominate the national government. President Nazarbaev is from this grouping. However, clan ties are only a minor factor behind the southerners' predominance. Kazakhs from the senior *zhuz* are more likely to succeed because they are from a wealthier region than their brethren in the junior *zhuz* and less subject to Russian domination than their confreres in the middle *zhuz*. The more numerous southerners also are closer to the capital.

Interethnic Relations and the Geographic Split

The greatest challenge to the republic's status quo aside from economic discontent lies in the relations between the Kazakhs and the slightly smaller ethnic Russian population, who comprise 41.9 percent and 37 percent of the population, respectively.[1] Russians dominate the industrial, mineral-rich northern and eastern regions along the border with the Russian Federation, and they run Kazakhstan's industry. The bulk of the ethnic Kazakh population is along the country's southern tier and in the far western regions, although these areas have some ethnic Russians in the urban centers and Russians are the majority in Almaty. In western Kazakhstan, rural areas dominated by Kazakhs are interspersed with oil-drilling towns populated almost entirely by Russians.

ethnic breakdown
Kazakh, 41.9%
Russian, 37.0%
Ukrainian, 5.2%
German, 4.7%
Uzbek, 2.1%
Tatar, 2.0%
Other, 7.1%

Separated from the south by a wide swath of empty steppe, the north and east are tied to Russia's Siberian and Ural regions by geography, industry, and energy grids, whereas southern Kazakhstan shares an energy grid with the rest of Central Asia farther south. In contrast to other Central Asian republics

---

1. In addition to ethnic Russians, there are smaller Slav populations, most notably Ukrainians, that are similar to the Russians in cultural, social, and economic terms. Frequently, the Slav populations are lumped together as "Russian-speakers."

where Russians first arrived 150 years ago, Russians in some areas of northern and eastern Kazakhstan have been settled for up to three centuries. The potential for secessionist movements is thus significant, although the current political disarray in Russia proper makes such activities unlikely for now.

Many ethnic Russians feel that the precedence given to the Kazakh language in government is discriminatory; they also believe that Kazakhs receive preferential treatment in government personnel decisions and education. Kazakhs frequently counter that the Russian population's concerns stem from the psychological impact of suddenly becoming a minority. In the view of many Kazakhs, Russians are complaining about what is in fact an attempt to redress previous unfair policies, not discrimination. In particular, Nazarbaev has stated that the legal imposition of Kazakh is necessary to save the language from extinction after decades of Russification in government.

Russians are showing their anxiety mainly with their feet. Concerns about their status have contributed to a high rate of emigration, although hopes of better living standards have been the most important motivation. More than 100,000 (and perhaps as many as 300,000) Russians out of about 6 million total emigrated in each of 1992 and 1993. (The net total has been reduced by immigration from other former Soviet republics as well as the return of some emigrants.)

Demography heightens the urgency of ethnic politics. Kazakhs have high birth rates and a low median age, whereas the ethnic Russians have a low birth rate and an older population that continues to diminish owing to emigration. The Kazakh population will be in a position to absorb ethnic Russians in a generation or two. Geographic absorption of the Russian north and east will be furthered if the government carries out its plan to move the capital from Almaty in the extreme southeast to Aqmola in the north. This will bind the Russian-dominated northern oblasts more firmly to the state of Kazakhstan and also prompt an influx of Kazakhs into the area.

Nazarbaev's government has made a concentrated effort to emphasize ethnic harmony within the republic (although reportedly stressing the issue more in the Russian-language media than in statements for Kazakh audiences). Assuming that Kazakhstan continues to develop as an independent state, its people, Russians included, will increasingly identify themselves with it, particularly if stability is maintained and the economy turns around. Nazarbaev frequently forwards the notion of a *Kazakhstani* identity free of ethnic affiliation. In many ways the republic's future depends on whether the notion sticks.

ECONOMICS

Material Assets Profile

Kazakhstan is endowed with vast hydrocarbon and mineral resources. The country possesses tens of billions of barrels in oil reserves located mostly in its western regions and its Caspian Sea shelf. It also has large coal mines in the north. Aside from these fossil fuels, there are significant deposits of copper, zinc, lead, bauxites, chromites, iron, silver, and gold, and large phosphate mines and fertilizer processing plants in the south around the city of Zhambul. All these industries are in need of additional investment and upgrading.

Kazakhstan boasts extensive agricultural production; it is the only exporter of wheat among the former Soviet republics, and also exports meat and some vegetables. It is a major producer of wool and leather.

The country has a highly developed heavy-machinery industry, mostly tied into the old Soviet defense complex, in the north and east. This industry is a mixed blessing as much of it consists of bloated dinosaur plants built by Soviet planners. They are invariably polluters and often produce something less valuable than the component raw materials. Despite this, the government is loath to attempt to reform the management of these plants for fear of the social consequences of unemployment. The economic problem has a strong ethnic component in that the plants are run almost entirely by Russians. Thus, reforms such as privatization have been limited to those plants most likely to succeed.

Performance in 1993

Kazakhstan remained in economic crisis in 1993 as it attempted to cope with the transition to a market economy and the economic problems related to the USSR's dissolution. The year witnessed a 15.9 percent fall in industrial production relative to 1992 (on top of a 13.8 percent fall in 1992) and a 13 percent fall in GDP. Much of the fall in GDP is inevitable as inefficient factories that produce goods for which there is little demand (particularly in the defense industry) either close or restructure. Moreover, annual extraction of coal and crude oil both fell by 12 percent, and continuing difficulties over exports and payments with Russia have soured the outlook for 1994.

There have been several positive trends in Kazakhstan's economy. Kazakhstan has begun to privatize. Virtually all dwellings are now privately owned. The government sold 153 small-scale enterprises in auctions in 1993, and it hopes to sell up to 5,000 in 1994. The government has also embarked on the privatization of 38 large plants in the country, mostly in the extractive and raw-material processing industries. In one instance, Philip Morris provided foreign investment by buying into a privatized tobacco factory. President Nazarbaev has also called for more active privatization of agricultural land, although progress remains slow.

The inflation rate was over 2000 percent in 1993, while the population's income increased in rouble terms by only 1000 percent. However, officials believe that administrative reform (including more open review of the government's books) among the economy-related ministries and the central bank will ensure tighter control over credit emissions and hence cut the rate of inflation, perhaps to 600 percent in 1994.

Perhaps the single most important event in Kazakhstan in 1993 was the introduction of its own currency, the *tenge*, on November 15. Having long advocated maintaining the rouble as a common currency for the CIS, Nazarbaev's government rejected Russia's conditions for providing the currency as an unacceptable surrender of sovereignty and hastily underwent the switch. The measure was not popular because it was accompanied by limitations on the amount of Soviet roubles that could be exchanged for the new currency,[2] delays in the payment of salaries and pensions in *tenge*, and a concomitant jump in the cost of state goods. Although the *tenge* has not fared well against the rouble and the dollar, it will have the long-term benefit of freeing Kazakhstan from the vagaries of Russia's own monetary policies. It is an important step toward true sovereignty.

Non-CIS Involvement

The most important positive development in Kazakhstan in 1993 was its success in attracting foreign investment needed to tap its natural and labor assets. In this regard Kazakhstan has done far better than its Central Asian neighbors and, relative to population, than Russia itself. Kazakhstan's state oil concern and Chevron concluded a landmark 40-year joint venture deal in 1993 that could bring up to $20 billion into Kazakhstan. The deal is the largest involving a foreign entity anywhere in the former Soviet Union, though Chevron has recently had to scale back the rate of investment because of problems with Russia over transporting the oil. Kazakhstan also signed a deal with a consortium of seven Western oil companies including Mobil to explore the Caspian Sea shelf. The combined assets of the seven companies make the consortium the largest ever in the world. British Petroleum and Italy's Agip have struck large separate deals to develop oil and gas fields.

Out of the more than 1,000 joint ventures registered by the end of 1993 between Kazakhstani and non-CIS partners, the largest number (more than 300) involve Chinese entities. For the most part these are very small trading ventures that bring in little investment. In terms of numbers of joint ventures, Turkish involvement ranks second, with over 150 joint ventures and more than 20 representative offices. Turkish firms have focused on leather goods, consumer electronics, and construction. The United States is the third largest partner in terms of numbers of firms engaged in

---

2. Kazakhstanis were allowed to trade in up to 100,000 Soviet roubles (roughly $35) in cash with no limitations. Amounts over this had to be accompanied by proof that the roubles had been earned legally. Also, owing to a primitive and at times confiscatory banking system, it was common for people to keep significant cash assets at home.

Kazakhstan, with over 60, and the largest in terms of capital flows into the country.

FOREIGN RELATIONS

President Nazarbaev has vigorously sought to promote multilateral structures that will provide economic and strategic stability in the chaotic post-Soviet environment. Among the leaders of former Soviet republics, he has been the most prominent advocate of coordinating policies within the CIS in order to limit the economic dislocation caused by the Soviet Union's breakup. Although Nazarbaev has proposed security arrangements in addition to those of the CIS, he has repeatedly stressed the importance of the CIS collective security treaty and strategic closeness to Russia.

Parallel to his support for CIS integration, Nazarbaev attaches special importance to Kazakhstan's relations with Russia. Given the CIS's lack of effective coordination and Russia's domination of the bloc's economic and security arrangements, these bilateral relations are in fact more important than ties to the commonwealth. Furthermore, Russia's huge role in Kazakhstan's interethnic relations and economy means that close, cooperative relations are not a policy choice but a necessity for Almaty.

Kazakhstan has agreed to transfer the 104 SS-18 nuclear missiles located on its territory to Russia for dismantlement by the year 2003 under the START-II treaty and has joined the Nuclear Nonproliferation Treaty as a non-nuclear nation. As of February 1994, Russia had removed its Tu-95 (Bear) strategic bombers stationed in airfields in Kazakhstan. The republic's non-nuclear stance is partly a renunciation of geopolitical ambitions and partly a necessity, since Kazakhstan lacks the resources to control or service a nuclear arsenal.

Despite the shared interest that Russia and Kazakhstan have in close links—or perhaps owing to the very depth of interests that tie the two countries together and preclude alternatives—friction grew during the fall of 1993 and winter of 1994. First, Kazakhstan and Russia have still not agreed on the amount of compensation the former should receive for the nuclear fuel obtained from its dismantled weapons. The two countries were long at loggerheads over the status of the Baikonur rocket-launch facility—the Cape

Canaveral of the Soviet space industry—located in Kazakhstan but run by scientists from Russia. Wrangling over this and payment for ecological damage strained relations for several months. Russia's breakup of the rouble zone was a slap in the face to Nazarbaev and caused a good deal of anger among Kazakhstan's population, which felt that it had been unfairly cut adrift. Finally, Moscow's repeated arrogation of special rights for Kazakhstan's ethnic Russian population has been a huge irritant to the Nazarbaev government.

Things went from bad to worse when Russian Foreign Minister Andrei Kozyrev visited Almaty in mid-November 1993 expressly to raise the issue of ethnic Russians' rights. Nazarbaev declined to meet him, citing a mysterious ailment, and had Prime Minister Sergei Tereschenko (himself an ethnic Ukrainian) receive Kozyrev instead. Tereschenko proceeded to turn the tables on the Russian foreign minister by pressing him on the status of the 600,000 ethnic Kazakhs within the Russian Federation.

Over the first three months of 1994, these problems grew more acute and new problems, such as Russia's suspension of fuel deliveries and Kazakhstan's retaliation, arose. Nazarbaev then went on a ten-day visit to the United States in mid-February that was widely viewed in Moscow as an attempt to gain leverage against Russia, although Kazakhstan's president vigorously denied this upon his return.

Nazarbaev suddenly changed the tenor of relations in a Moscow summit with Russia's Boris Yeltsin on March 29 and 30, 1994, by making major concessions to Russia. Among the twenty agreements signed, two stand out. First, Russia received a 20-year lease with a possible 10-year extension on the Baikonur rocket-launch facility for a payment of $115 million per year, far below the reported $7 billion per year that Almaty wanted. Second, Almaty reportedly agreed to provide shares of its state drilling company to its Russian counterpart for joint exploitation of oil located in Kazakhstan's Caspian Sea shelf. In return for these concessions, Moscow reportedly agreed to desist from pressing the dual citizenship issue. The strongest statement yet of Kazakhstan's commitment to close relations with Russia was Nazarbaev's pitch for a Eurasian Union of the former Soviet republics, with Russia and Kazakhstan at its core.

Behind Nazarbaev's conciliatory attitude was an understanding of the crucial need for good relations with Russia and, secondarily, a sense of increasing isolation. The leaders of Turkmenistan, the Kyrgyz Republic, and Uzbekistan had all met with Yeltsin in the preceding three months to reconfirm their strategic closeness, strengthen bilateral economic agreements, and pledge to work for the betterment of their countries' ethnic Russians. Nazarbaev could ill afford to be odd man out in dealings with Russia.

Kazakhstan has also explored the formulation of foreign relations that take into account new geopolitical opportunities. There have been some mostly declarative moves to integrate within Central Asia, most notably when the five republics signed an agreement to create a Union of Central Asian Peoples on January 5, 1993, in Tashkent. In January 1994, Kazakhstan together with the Kyrgyz Republic and Uzbekistan created a single economic zone that provides for the unimpeded movement of goods, services, capital, and labor among the three countries. Although there is an element of rivalry between Kazakhstan and Uzbekistan, they presented a united front to preserve the rouble zone and worked together to coordinate the introduction of their own currencies.

Kazakhstan endorses the Economic Cooperation Organization, mainly as a potential means of exporting its mineral resources to the world at large. Nazarbaev has also launched an initiative to create a mutual security agreement, the Conference on Interaction and Confidence Building Measures in Asia, though at present it consists of little more than a series of general statements by Kazakhstan's leadership about the need to prevent conflicts in the region collectively. Two meetings of experts from foreign ministries have been held to work out an agenda for a session of foreign ministers to discuss such a security arrangement.[3]

Kazakhstan has sought warmer political relations with China, although the latter's policies on nuclear testing and issues of Tur-

---

3. The last meeting of experts was held August 30–September 1, 1993, in Almaty. Experts attended from Afghanistan, Azerbaijan, China, India, Iran, Israel, Kazakhstan, the Kyrgyz Republic, North Korea, Mongolia, the Palestine Liberation Organization, Pakistan, the Russian Federation, Syria, Tajikistan, Turkey, Uzbekistan, and Vietnam. Observers attended from Australia, Cambodia, Japan, Indonesia, South Korea, Thailand, Turkmenistan, the United Nations, the CSCE, the League of Arab States, and the Islamic Conference Organization.

kic nationalism in Xinjiang Region have been hindrances. Trade has boomed, but many in Kazakhstan resent the small-scale Chinese traders who have entered the republic's markets selling goods of poor quality. Nonetheless, Kazakhstan's government recognizes the importance of workable relations with its enormous, economically growing eastern neighbor.

Finally, Kazakhstan has actively sought attention from the West, as was most recently demonstrated by Nazarbaev's visit to the United States in February 1994. Kazakhstan eagerly seeks Western investment like that which Chevron has promised to develop its economy. In addition, strong relations with the West help bolster the country in its dealings with Russia.

These efforts to broaden Kazakhstan's non-CIS ties remain secondary to its relationship with Russia. Despite the rancor of the fall of 1993 and fears raised by increased Russian nationalism, Kazakhstan presently has no alternative but to continue its Russia-oriented foreign policy. Since Russia's greater size and power make it the protagonist, the key issue is what kind of relations a politically inchoate Moscow wants to establish. Kazakhstan is eager for as much economic cooperation as possible without forfeiting full state sovereignty, but, as Nazarbaev himself noted in February, "It takes two to tango."[4] And Kazakhstan's partner has shown a penchant for taking an unwanted, interventionist lead.

---

4. *Izvestiya*, February 23, 1994.

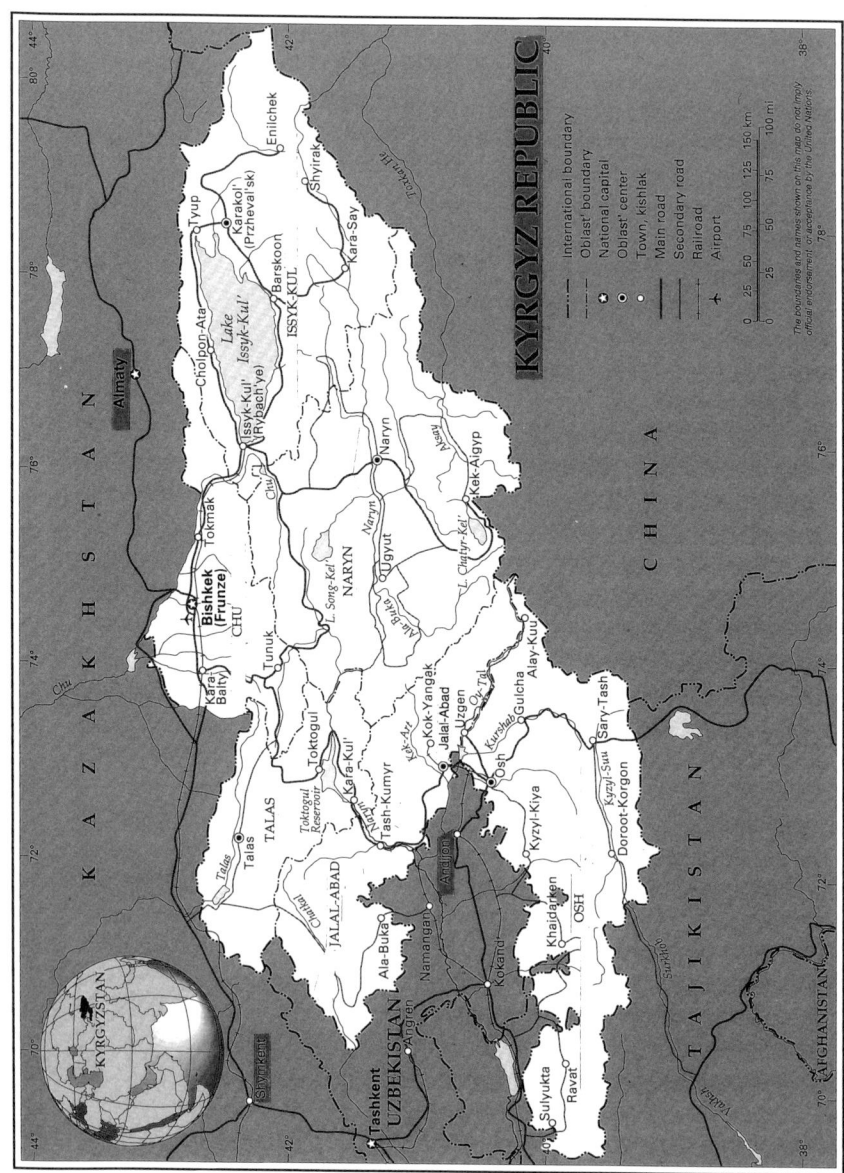

THE KYRGYZ REPUBLIC

POLITICS

President Askar Akaev

The Kyrgyz Republic, often known as Kyrgyzstan or by its old Soviet name of Kirgizia, is entering its most stable period as a sovereign state. Post-independence politics were pervaded by contention between reform-minded President Askar Akaev and members of the old Communist-era elite who dominate parliament and other government structures. However, after a year of often turbulent political debates and standoffs in 1993, Akaev emerged with newfound support among the old administrative class and a huge referendum victory in January 1994.

Akaev had an impressive academic career as a professor of physics, eventually becoming president of the Kyrgyz Academy of Sciences in 1989. Although he joined the Communist Party of the Soviet Union in 1981 and became a member of the Central Committee of the Kyrgyz Communist Party in July 1990, he is not associated with the old *nomenklatura* (elite). His rapid rise within the party—which was still synonymous with the government even at the end of the Soviet period—was thanks largely to support from General Secretary Mikhail Gorbachev in Moscow. This support was based on the fact that Akaev was a reform-minded intellectual who contrasted with the conservative Communist bureaucracy. Akaev assumed leadership of the republic in October 1990, after the old *nomenklatura* had split and its leaders had been discredited by their handling of disturbances between Uzbeks and Kyrgyz in the country's south a few months earlier.

Upon achieving power, Akaev promoted civil liberties and made deeper inroads into the Communist Party's hold over power than any other Central Asian leader. Although some newspapers complained of obstruction in the lead-up to the 1994 referendum, the media remains essentially uncensored. Political parties ranging from communist to nationalist function freely, often holding demonstrations and criticizing Akaev and others in government.

While Akaev's anti-*nomenklatura* stance has won praise at home and abroad, his support for civil liberties has not provided a strong base of power, particularly in light of the mounting public preoccupation with the country's economic difficulties. His main source of strength has been among the intelligentsia, specifically his colleagues from the Academy of Sciences, some of whom have even assumed government positions. At the same time, Akaev has faced political opposition, at a level unthinkable in other Central Asian states, from the leadership of the Communist Party and government administrators from the Soviet era.

Members of the old bureaucratic elite have a large presence in the country's parliament, the *Jogorku Kenesh*, the deputies of which were elected in 1990 when the Communist Party still ruled supreme. Not surprisingly, the parliament has challenged Akaev and his government on a number of his initiatives, although in key instances, such as the adoption of a constitution in early May 1993 and the subsequent introduction of a new currency, it ultimately went along with Akaev's wishes. The strongest attack came during the fall of 1993, when the legislature used a scandal over the disappearance of some of the country's gold reserves to cast doubts upon Akaev's competence and the honesty of some of his associates, particularly his loyal prime minister, Tursunbek Chyngyshev. In a stormy parliamentary session in December 1993, deputies forced Chyngyshev to resign and voted on a list of recommended replacements; significantly, former Kyrgyz Communist Party First Secretary Absamat Masaliev was at the top of the list. Akaev was further weakened by the resignation and defection to the critics' camp of his already estranged but independently powerful vice president, Felix Kulov.

Akaev resigned himself to working more closely with the Soviet-era administrative caste. He replaced Chyngyshev with Apas Jumagulov, second on the parliament's list of candidates and the last Communist prime minister but a politically unchallenging figure, who was quickly confirmed by the parliament. Akaev also called on the elements of the old Communist Party to help govern the country.

Four days prior to the opening of the December 1993 parliamentary session, Akaev announced that there would be a vote of confidence in his presidency on January 30, 1994. Although the official reason for the measure was that Akaev needed to reconfirm his presidential powers after the adoption of the new constitution, the timing of the announcement suggests that he was appealing to popular support in order to meet the challenges posed by the parliament to his authority. According to official results, Akaev received 96 percent of the ballots cast (with over 96 percent of the registered population participating). While there are doubts raised by the magnitude of his victory, the referendum was a shot in the arm for Akaev. The vote also reflected the endorsement of local officials who campaigned on his behalf.

Clans

An important element in the republic's political landscape is the influence of clans based upon the tribal and regional divisions among the Kyrgyz population. Although it is difficult for an outsider to assess the extent to which clans determine decision-making in the country, regionalism is reputedly quite important in at least low- and mid-level personnel choices and in dealing out state contracts and construction projects.

The two major regions of the republic are the north (composed of the city of Bishkek, Chu Oblast, Issyk-Kul Oblast, and Talas Oblast) and the south (consisting of Osh Oblast and Jalal-Abad Oblast). Naryn Oblast, a poor, remote region along the border with China, does not fall into either category. The north and south are divided by the Tian Shan mountain range, which is impassable for a few months of the year. Both regions have roughly 2 million people, but the north has a much higher proportion of Europeans (mostly Russians) and is generally more prosperous, with a higher concentration of industry. Most of the republic's political elite, past and present, hail from the north. The south is culturally and economically a part of the Fergana Valley (most of which is in Uzbekistan) and has a significant Uzbek minority. The two areas are culturally distinct, although both are dominated by ethnic Kyrgyz.

There is some resentment in the south of its lower living standards and perceived neglect. Parliamentary deputies from Osh and Jalal-Abad oblasts have spoken of creating a "Southern Party" to protect their exclusive interests, and there have even been isolated calls to make Osh the capital in order to channel more state funds to the south. Nonetheless, the north-south differentiation does not at present seem likely to result in anything more than pork-barrel politics between the two regions over central government allocations.

The Akaev government is very conscious of the potential for internal divisions. It has made several gestures to consolidate national unity, including the establishment of a branch of the Academy of Sciences in Jalal-Abad. Akaev has even called for burrowing a railroad through the Tian Shan mountains to connect the country's two halves, though the republic will not be able to afford this extremely expensive venture any time soon.

The north and south are subdivided into regional clans that correspond to the republic's oblasts. President Akaev is from the Kemin district of Chu Oblast; the perception among some that people from his clan are benefiting unduly from this circumstance has led to the quip that the republic has gone from "Communism to Keminism."

Interethnic Relations

In contrast to the behind-the-scenes influence of clans in Kyrgyz politics, ethnic relations have captured much attention, particularly from abroad. This issue concerns the two major ethnic minorities in the Kyrgyz Republic: Russians and Uzbeks. Russians make up about one-fifth of the country's population and are concentrated in the city of Bishkek and the surrounding Chu Valley. City-dwelling Uzbeks make up about one-quarter of the south's total population but a much higher proportion of the region's urban centers.

Russians' complaints are similar to those made in other Central Asian republics: a perceived ethnic bias in government appointments; the establishment of Kyrgyz alone as the official state language and the elimination of the Russian language in government affairs by the year 2000 (one of the fastest rates of transition in Central Asia); and uncertainty over their children's future in an increasingly Kyrgyz-dominated country. Some small Russian-oriented movements have sprung up in response to these challenges. The greatest expression of Russian anxiety was the resignation and emigration of the leading Russian in government, Deputy Prime Minister German Kuznetsov, in June 1993. Kuznetsov declared that there was no place for Slavs in the country.

Unhappiness among the Russian population of the Kyrgyz Republic has contributed to the highest rate of emigration relative to population in Central Asia after that of war-torn Tajikistan. Nonetheless, ethnic anxieties are generally not the most important motive for emigration; rather, the chief concern of the republic's citizens, Russian and Kyrgyz alike, has been the country's economic downslide. Russians feel that economic prospects are sufficiently better in Russia to warrant pulling up stakes. According to Kyrgyz officials, about 100,000 Russians left per year in 1992 and 1993 out of a population of a little over 900,000 ethnic Russians. However, up to a quarter of the emigrants have returned, having found it difficult to get work and adapt in Russia.

ethnic breakdown
Kyrgyz, 52.4%
Russian, 21.5%
Uzbek, 12.9%
Ukrainian, 2.5%
German, 2.4%
Tatar, 1.6%
Other, 6.6%

The departure of the Russians has dealt a blow to the country's already ailing economy. Recognizing that the republic's industrial backbone is composed of Russians, the Akaev government has taken several steps to stem emigration. The most notable measures have been the establishment of a Slavic university in Bishkek to provide higher education exclusively in Russian and the recent establishment of a joint Kyrgyz-Russian enterprise support fund that will use money from Moscow to buttress industries run mainly by Russians. Akaev even spoke of instituting dual citizenship with Russia, although legislation expressly forbids it; he has since backed off from the idea. While earning criticism from Kyrgyz nationalists, these measures have reduced the pressure from Moscow to shore up the ethnic Russians' rights.

Relations between Uzbeks and Kyrgyz are calm, although just four years ago the two ethnic groups clashed in the southern cities of Osh and Uzgen. While the genesis of the conflict can be traced far back into the two peoples' histories, the recent tension stemmed from rising Kyrgyz discontent with the near monopoly of markets by Uzbeks as the economy declined and hidden unemployment grew in the late 1980s. In addition, Uzbeks were unhappy with Kyrgyz domination of government structures, particularly when new officials were installed in the spring of 1990. Friction was heightened by calls from the Uzbek minority in March of that year to make the south an Uzbek autonomous region within the Kyrgyz Republic.

A dispute over the distribution of land plots in the city of Osh in June 1990 finally sparked open strife. Rumors of atrocities aroused members of both groups to take up arms in their own areas or travel to Osh or Uzgen to fight for their brethren. After several days of vicious street fighting, order was restored with the help of the Soviet Army. At least scores, and perhaps hundreds, died, mostly in Uzgen.

Many of the factors that led to the 1990 conflict have since subsided. The Kyrgyz-Uzbek dichotomy in trade and government has become less pronounced. The wave of nationalist sentiment that arose under glasnost in the Soviet Union's last years has passed. Finally, and most important in terms of precluding a repetition, local observers believe that the brutality of the clash sobered both populations enough to avoid confrontation in the future.

Ethnic and clan divisions within the republic's body politic do not at present pose a serious challenge to the country's political equilibrium. Akaev is solidly in control after the January 1994 referendum. Furthermore, the fact that divisions have remained within the bounds of parliamentary debates and maneuvering rather than erupting into open conflict indicates underlying national stability born of responsible politics (one need only compare the consequences of similar divisions in Tajikistan in 1992 or Russia in 1993).

ECONOMICS

Material Assets Profile

The Kyrgyz Republic has major deposits of gold. Home to one of the first Soviet mines, the republic has begun to exploit new fields, largely with foreign investment. About 20 tons of gold were mined in 1993, and other fields will be put to a tender in 1994. The republic also possesses significant deposits of rare earth metals, in particular chrome, mercury, uranium, and antimony. Aside from metals, it contains basalt, marble, and other ornamental stones used in construction.

The country is almost entirely reliant on oil from Russia and natural gas from Uzbekistan. Its own resources are limited and virtually inaccessible. The general downturn and chaotic disruptions in CIS trade, particularly of fuel deliveries, have led to periodic shortages. These have frequently crippled airports and have brought several industrial plants to a standstill.

On the other hand, with mountains making up 95 percent of its countryside, the republic has a largely untapped potential for producing hydroelectric power. It hopes to replace its thermal electricity plants, which require fuel imports, and increase exports of power to neighboring regions, primarily Uzbekistan. Kyrgyz hydroelectric power plants in the southwest already supply the Fergana Valley with electricity on both sides of the border with Uzbekistan. Unfortunately, the country suffers from a severe shortage of capital to invest in this sector; construction on three dams has been halted owing to lack of funds.

The ruggedness of the terrain limits cultivation. Some wheat is planted in the Chu and Talas river valleys in the north, and cotton, fruits, and vegetables are grown in the thin outer strip of the Fergana Valley lying within the Kyrgyz Republic. Most vegetables and grains, as well as fodder for intensive livestock breeding, are imported. These imports are also subject to disruptions caused by the instability of trade among the CIS states. Consequent fodder shortages have forced a reduction of herds for the past several years. In 1993 alone, cattle herds declined by one-fifth and goat and sheep herds by one-quarter.

The Kyrgyz people traditionally were nomadic herders, and animal husbandry remains an important part of their economy.

Even with recent losses, the republic has nearly as many sheep and goats as there are people. The country is a net exporter of meat, mostly to Uzbekistan, and of leather.

The country's small industrial base is concentrated in textiles and metallurgy. There are some industrial plants tied into the old Soviet defense complex, including a uranium enrichment facility in Issyk-Kul Oblast.

The republic's spectacular, mostly pristine mountain terrain and the Issyk-Kul Lake (2,355 square miles located more than 5,000 feet above sea level) can potentially be a draw for tourism, although this will require heavy investment in infrastructure.

Performance in 1993

The Kyrgyz Republic continued to experience severe economic dislocation in 1993. According to official sources, GDP fell by 13.4 percent (after a fall of 16.4 percent in 1992), while the consumer price index rose by about 1500 percent. Industrial production fell by nearly a quarter (after a similar drop in 1992), the steepest decline among the Central Asian republics. The republic will continue to face very high levels of industrial decline as a result of chronic fuel shortages, high levels of emigration by ethnic Russian industrial workers, and dependence on exports to other CIS states.

The Akaev government responded to these pressures by aggressively pursuing economic reforms. In doing so, it has been receptive to advice from the International Monetary Fund (IMF), the World Bank, and other Western sources.

The republic's most prominent reform in 1993 was the introduction of its own currency, the *som*, on May 10. With prompting from the IMF, the Akaev government made this decision to garner more economic support from the West and to avoid being at the whim of the Russian Central Bank (a prescient policy, as became clear when Uzbekistan and Kazakhstan had to abandon the rouble in haste). President Akaev pushed the decision through the legislature in anticipation of a meeting of the IMF's board of directors in New York on May 13. The country was rewarded: the IMF has since disbursed $62 million to help stabilize the *som*.

The move was not without its detractors. Public discontent ran high as prices were doubled and the state withheld salaries, pensions, stipends, and payments for several weeks. The exchange process for old Soviet roubles did not run smoothly either. Rural areas were still reportedly short of cash in early 1994. However, on the positive side, the *som* with its IMF backing has proved to be the most stable of the Central Asian currencies.

The governments of neighboring Uzbekistan and Kazakhstan protested the move, noting that the republic had not adequately forewarned them as required by CIS agreements. Both countries closed their borders with the Kyrgyz Republic to staunch the flow of Kyrgyz citizens who sought to dump their roubles. The closure of borders was also an expression of irritation by Presidents Karimov and Nazarbaev over the fact that the much smaller Kyrgyz Republic, led by a politically inexperienced Akaev, jumped ahead of them on currency issues and undercut their stance on preserving the rouble zone. Akaev went to Tashkent and Almaty to smooth out relations, apologizing for not having properly informed his neighbors, though not before he had been to the United States to ensure financial backing for the *som*.

The government has shown a strong commitment to the creation of a private sector. Privatization of enterprises was begun soon after independence, in the first quarter of 1992, and over a quarter of state assets had been privatized by October 1, 1993, mostly in the construction and service sectors. Almost all dwellings have been privatized. The country plans to privatize several large enterprises, including mines and energy plants, after a period of parallel state management beginning in 1994.

Throughout 1992 and 1993 privatization was authorized and supervised on a case-by-case basis by a special state property fund, rather than according to a rigid set of regulations. In general, the incumbent state-appointed managers have been the beneficiaries of privatization. There reportedly was some corruption as interested parties sought to influence the property fund's decision-making. In response to calls to open up the process and make it fairer, the government distributed vouchers to the population good for the purchase of shares of corporatized enterprises beginning in 1994.

Agricultural reform has been much slower, although individual leasing of land for life has been promoted, resulting in the creation of some 15,000 farms. Land is a sensitive issue in the country since so little of it is suitable for cultivation. After all, it was a dispute over land rights that triggered the disturbances in Osh in 1990. Most land remains state-owned.

Non-CIS Involvement

The Kyrgyz Republic's efforts to implement political and economic reform have won praise and support from Western governments and international economic bodies. Turkey, the United States, the European Union, and Japan have technical assistance programs and provide loans to buy food products. The country is the highest per capita recipient of U.S. governmental aid of any former Soviet republic.

However, despite public support, private business has shown little interest in the country. The most important success has been two ventures with Canadian partners to exploit some of the republic's gold mines. The largest number of joint ventures (about 75) is with Chinese partners, but these mostly involve small-scale trading. Turkey is second in number of joint ventures, mainly in the wool and leather industries. Only a few relatively small joint ventures bring investment to consumer goods manufacturing.

The low level of interest is not for lack of trying; the Kyrgyz Republic has eagerly promoted foreign investment by legislative and other means. However, companies seeking new markets tend to look toward the larger, more resource-rich countries to the north and west. Many of the Kyrgyz Republic's natural assets are difficult to access, and the difficulty of travel to and within the country discourages investment.

FOREIGN RELATIONS

As a small country lacking many key resources, the Kyrgyz Republic must seek good relations with its three much larger and more powerful partners, Russia, Kazakhstan, and Uzbekistan. Akaev has stated that relations with these nations and more generally the CIS is "the unconditional priority in our foreign policy, and it will remain the main priority over the next decade."[1]

---

1. *Slovo Kyrgyzstana*, October 12, 1993.

Akaev's gestures toward ethnic Russians and especially his flirtation with the idea of dual citizenship have sweetened the relationship with Russia. Moscow's economic ministers welcomed the introduction of the *som* as easing the burden on the rouble. Members of Moscow's political establishment are pleased by Akaev's support for integration under the CIS, especially his statement that the introduction of the *som* is a logical step to ultimate monetary integration into a new rouble zone.

The Kyrgyz Republic enjoys good relations with Kazakhstan and Uzbekistan, although they have not always been smooth. As noted above, there was friction over the *som*'s introduction. Tashkent has also been disgruntled when politicians and journalists, often from the Uzbek opposition, have been allowed to criticize Uzbekistan's politics from the Kyrgyz Republic; in particular, a scandal arose when Uzbekistani secret police abducted an Uzbek oppositionist attending a human rights conference in Bishkek in June 1992. Nonetheless, these tensions are small disturbances in an otherwise reasonably smooth trilateral relationship. Aside from common Turkic heritage, the three countries are bound by economic and strategic logic in that they face common problems of geography and post-Soviet dislocation. After entering into agreements in Tashkent on January 5, 1993, to create the Union of Central Asian Peoples, the three republics signed another treaty in January 1994 to remove all barriers to the flow of capital, goods, services, and labor.

The Kyrgyz Republic has a special interest in promoting a stable Tajikistan. Thousands of the 60,000 ethnic Kyrgyz in Tajikistan crossed into the Kyrgyz Republic to flee the fighting. In addition, a key road from Khorog, on the Tajikistan-Afghanistan border, to Osh reportedly serves as a major conduit for smuggled goods, especially narcotics. Yet the two countries have still not formally established bilateral relations since achieving independence; bitter and at times bloody disagreements over water issues in the Fergana Valley led to delays in concluding the agreement, which were compounded when Tajikistan slid into civil conflict. Nonetheless, several interregional agreements including accords between Osh Oblast and Badakhshon in Tajikistan have been signed. The Kyrgyz Republic covers 10 percent of the operating costs of the joint CIS forces in Tajikistan and has contributed a battalion of troops; the initiative for this measure came from Russia.

The opportunity to deal directly with the outside world following independence has led to increased contacts with China, South Asia, and linguistically related Turkey. The basis for the growing relationships is almost exclusively trade. In particular, Chinese traders have been extremely active in filling the republic's consumer markets and buying property. Turkey has been active in deepening cultural contacts, but the republic remains firmly within Russia's orbit.

As a champion of reform and civil liberties in a region of authoritarian regimes, Akaev has succeeded in attracting economic assistance and public support from the West. Yet Akaev knows which side the bread is buttered on: economically and strategically, the relationships with the local great power—Russia—are the deepest and most important.

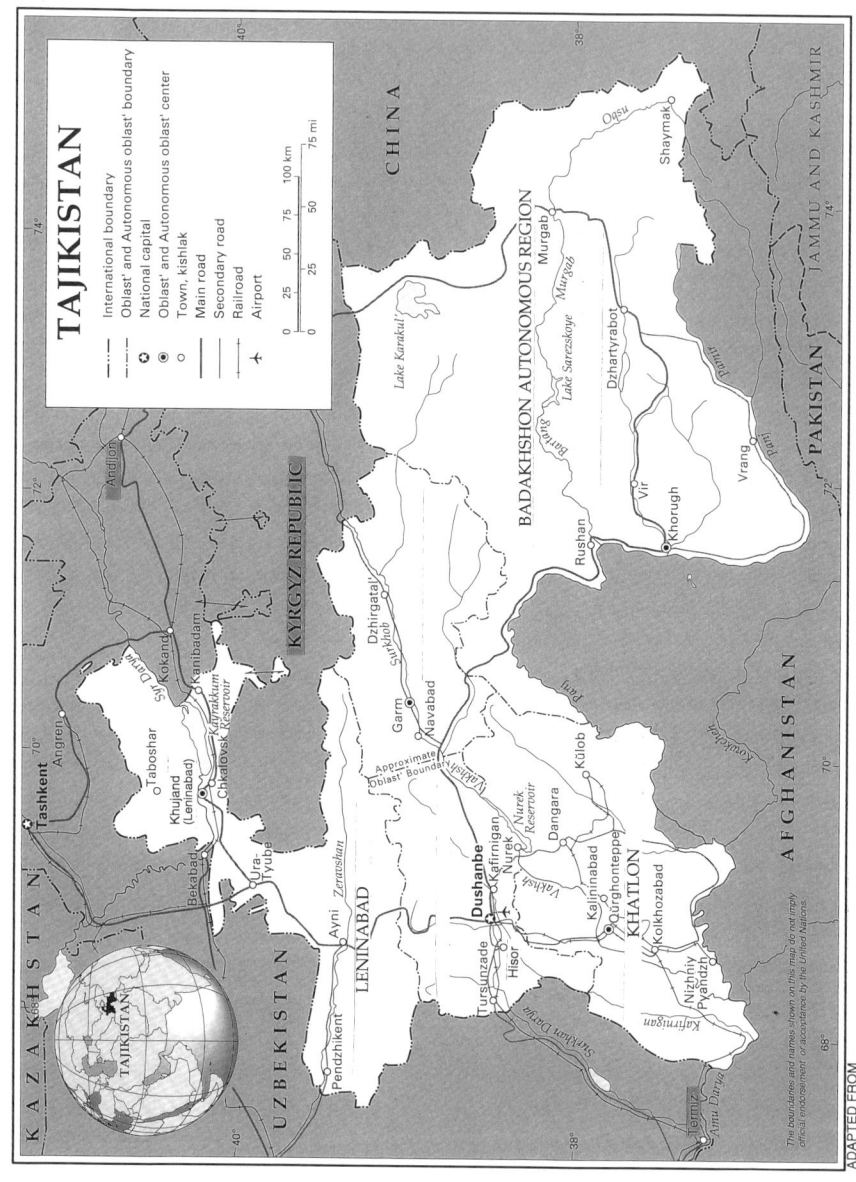

TAJIKISTAN

POLITICS

Tajikistan's politics bear the heavy stamp of the republic's brutal civil war, which took place in the second half of 1992 and early 1993. Although large-scale hostilities ceased by February 1993 and major towns are relatively calm, sporadic fighting continues. Even before the shooting started, Tajikistan had the weakest economy of all the republics in the former Soviet Union; the war devastated it. Tajikistan's government has been forced to sacrifice independence for semi-protectorate status under Moscow in order to get Russian military support and keep its economy afloat.

The many causes of the conflict read like a register of political variables in post-independence Central Asia gone awry: an ideological conflict between an opposition of Islamic "fundamentalists" allied with "nationalists" and radical Democrats versus "neocommunists" who refused to relinquish their hold on power (as the various parties labeled each other with only partial accuracy); ethnic differences pitting Tajiks against Uzbeks and Uzbekistan; heavy-handed involvement by Russia in shaping politics; and, most important, regional clan rivalries submerging any sense of nationhood. Unfortunately, while the military victors in the civil war have a fairly secure hold over the central government (as long as Russia keeps providing support) and most of the shooting has stopped, the divisions in Tajikistan that led to the bloodshed remain unresolved.

Clan Divisions

Intense rivalries among the country's region-based clans lay at the core of the conflict and continue to be a determining force in Tajikistan's politics. Although one might expect that the Tajiks' Persian culture and language in largely Turkic Central Asia would unite them (and some nationalists have called for unity on these very grounds), they are in fact a divided people, identifying with their own locales far more than with the republic for which they are named.

Tajikistan's terrain, 93 percent of which is mountainous, lends itself to regional divisions. Two of the country's regions, Leninabad Oblast in the north and Badakhshon Autonomous Oblast in the southeast, are separated from the rest of the country during the winter, when 10,000-foot-high passes connecting the regions are snowed in. Mountains and the passes between them play an important role in isolating Tajikistan's other major distinct regions and their clans: the so-called Garm areas along the Karategin Valley to the east of the country's capital, Dushanbe; the Kulob region in the central south; and the Hisor Valley to the immediate west of Dushanbe.

Neither the Qurghonteppe region in the southwest (administratively joined together with Kulob in December 1992) nor the capital of Dushanbe and its immediate environs is home to a specific regional clan. These areas became densely populated only in the twentieth century. Soviet planners moved Garmis, Kulobis, and Badakhshonis into Qurghonteppe in the 1940s and 1950s to develop cotton production, throwing them into contact with Uzbeks and Central Asian Arabs who lived in the area. Before becoming the capital of Tajikistan in the 1920s, Dushanbe was just a small town. It grew to be a city of over half a million by the 1980s, when people from all over the republic as well as Russians from abroad came to the capital to take advantage of educational and employment opportunities. In moving, Tajiks retained a strong sense of loyalty to their home region and generally did not mix with other clans, while long-time inhabitants of Dushanbe and Qurghonteppe often identified themselves as Garmis, Kulobis, and so forth. Not surprisingly, much of the bloodiest fighting in the civil conflict came in these two areas, where regional clans rubbed shoulders with each other.

There are important social and economic differences among the regions. Leninabad Oblast emerged in the Soviet period as far and away the most populous, prosperous, and industrial region. Its relative prosperity has increased in the past two years since it did not suffer during the war. Surrounded on three sides by Uzbekistan, it has a large Uzbek minority and is economically far more interconnected with its northern neighbor than with the southern part of Tajikistan. Representatives of Leninabad Oblast historically dominated the Tajik Communist Party hierarchy, in large part explaining why the region fared much better than others.

Although the poorer southern regions historically share poverty and political isolation, they too are strongly divided. The Hisor Valley is a relatively well-off agricultural area, as was the Qurghonteppe region before the war. Both have significant Uzbek minorities. The Karategin Valley and Kulob are poorer, more mountainous, and more heavily Tajik. Kulobis emerged as junior partners to the Leninabadis in Communist Party structures in the 1970s.

Perched atop the Pamirs (a mountain range located mostly in Tajikistan), sparsely settled Badakhshon is the least developed region in the country and possibly anywhere in the former Soviet Union. The region imports almost all consumer goods and about 70 percent of its food. Badakhshonis speak a language distinct from Tajik and are Ismailis, whereas the rest of Tajikistan's indigenous population is Sunni by tradition. The region is reputedly a center for the production of narcotics as well as a transit route by which drugs from Afghanistan enter the CIS.

Ethnic Divisions

The other major ethnic group in Tajikistan's political mosaic is defined by ethno-linguistic characteristics rather than regional identity: the Uzbeks. Uzbeks make up about a quarter of the country's population and are concentrated in Leninabad Oblast, the Hisor Valley, and the Qurghonteppe region. Uzbeks and Tajiks in Leninabad Oblast and the Hisor Valley have lived together and intermarried for centuries. However, Uzbeks in Qurghonteppe did not mix with the Garmis and other Tajiks who moved to the area only decades ago.

Aside from their sheer numbers and supporting role in Leninabad Oblast, the Uzbeks' position in Tajikistan is important as part of the greater issue of Tajik-Uzbek relations. Uzbeks make up a significant minority in Tajikistan, and Tajiks do in Uzbekistan; moreover, some Tajiks consider the cities of Samarkand and Bukhara, now located in Uzbekistan, to be rightfully theirs. The significant Uzbek presence inevitably prompts involvement by larger neighboring Uzbekistan in Tajikistan's affairs.

ethnic breakdown:
Tajik, 64.9%
Uzbek, 25.0%
Russian, 3.5%
Tatar, 1.4%
Kyrgyz, 1.3%
Other, 3.9 %

The country's small Russian community accounted for 3.5 percent of the population in 1989, but two-thirds or more of the group fled during the war. Russians never played an active role in Tajikistan's regional or ethnic rivalries, since they viewed their domicile in association with Moscow's rule. Similar to the situation in other Central Asian republics, however, this population raises the issue of Russia's involvement on their behalf. Russia rationalizes its presence in Tajikistan by claiming to protect the Russian community, although there are also clear geopolitical motives for its involvement. Tajikistan's government has been accommodating to Moscow's concerns over its tiny ethnic Russian population, even considering ways of granting dual citizenship and continuing the use of the Russian language in government.

At its most basic level, the civil war was a struggle among clans: Kulobis and Hisoris with support from the Uzbeks and the Uzbekistani government and cheerleading by the Leninabadis defeated a combination of Garmis and Badakhshonis. The current central government is dominated by a sometimes uneasy coalition of the victorious Kulobis and Leninabadis. Naturally, politics and regional affiliation do not perfectly correspond, and clans are far from the only political force. For instance, persons from Leninabad Oblast are prominent leaders in the opposition and the current government includes Garmis and Badakhshonis, although none in very powerful positions. Many of the first victims of the war were Kulobis who supported the opposition. Nonetheless, the breakdown of the Soviet state led to the emergence of regional loyalties as the greatest indigenous political force in Tajikistan.

The Civil War

Tajikistan was the scene of political ferment in 1990 and 1991 as movements arose in opposition to the local Communist Party *nomenklatura*. Chief among these movements were: the Islamic Renaissance Party (IRP), inspired although not formally led by the republic's chief cleric, *Qazikolon* (Great Qazi) Akbar Turajonzoda; the Democratic Party (DP), which called for pluralism; *Rastokhez* (Rebirth), a movement of intellectuals who sought to make Tajik the official state language; and *La'le Badakhshon* (Ruby of Badakhshon), which sought more autonomy for the southeast region.

The most influential group was the IRP. Islam had retained a strong presence among the Tajik population despite 70 years of Soviet rule, and it served as an effective unifying force against ex-Communists who continued to hold power. The IRP claimed to advocate a gradual increase for Islam's role in society; its detractors denounced the party's supporters as *"Wahabi,"* a reference to the strict form of Islam prevalent in Saudi Arabia that connotes both extremism and foreign influence. The IRP had strongest grassroots support among the Garmi clan.

After independence from Moscow, the local Communist Party elite consolidated its grip on power in the republic. The former party first secretary, Rahmon Nabiev, won contested presidential elections in November 1991 with strong support from the state media and perhaps even outright manipulation of voting results. The Communist Party leadership then ousted the mayor of Dushanbe, who was associated with the opposition, and a Badakhshoni interior minister.

A loose alliance of opposition movements protested in early April 1992 by camping out in front of Dushanbe's main government building, demanding greater power-sharing and the reinstallment of these officials. Government supporters were bused into a counterdemonstration a quarter of a mile down the street later that month. The bloodshed began when shooting broke out between the opposition groups and the government's supporters on May 5. After a few days, the opposition groups prevailed, forcing Nabiev to form a coalition government in which they received 8 of 24 ministerial portfolios. Pro-opposition youths later forced Nabiev to resign at gunpoint in early September.

The events in Dushanbe sent shock waves across the country. Leninabad Oblast's officials refused to accept the new coalition government and cut their region off from the rest of the country. Kulob had generally been opposed to the IRP (in part owing to disagreements between the local clergy and the *Qazikolon*); the events in Dushanbe cemented the region's sentiments against the opposition. Determined not to let the opposition succeed, Kulobi clansmen formed the Popular Front, an army that received Uzbekistani support and acquired weapons from Russian Army units in the country. The front was led by Sangak Safarov, a convicted murderer who had spent 23 years in prison. Separate armed militias aligned against the opposition also sprang up in the Hisor Valley.

While sparked by political divisions, the conflict rapidly assumed a clan character. Increasingly brutal fighting and reported atrocities occurred in the Qurghonteppe region, where Kulobis and ethnic Uzbeks were pitted against Garmis and Badakhshonis. With a growing amount of Uzbekistani-supplied firepower, the Popular Front had prevailed in the area by November 1992. Meanwhile, the opposition in Dushanbe also faced a challenge from Safarali Kenjaev, the former chairman of the country's Supreme Soviet and acknowledged leader of the Hisori armed groups (although himself a Leninabadi). Kenjaev led an unsuccessful, bloody three-day attack on the capital in October. By the end of the month, the opposition movements were limited to control over the powerless central government in Dushanbe, itself subject to warlordism and banditry.

The Communist Party–dominated Supreme Soviet held a session in Khujand, Leninabad Oblast, in mid-November to reassert control over the country. With Popular Front leader Safarov working behind the scenes, the legislature sacked the government in Dushanbe and replaced it with a government dominated by Kulobis and Leninabadis. Although the IRP-DP alliance in Dushanbe agreed to step down and accept the new government, fighting continued. After several days of street battles, units of the Popular Front and the Hisori militias seized Dushanbe by force on December 11.

After taking the capital, the Popular Front chased the armed supporters of the IRP-DP alliance up the Karategin Valley east of

Dushanbe. By February 1994, the remaining opposition fighters were forced to flee across the Pamirs into Afghanistan. Popular Front units also swept through the Qurghonteppe region in the second half of December, taking revenge on presumed supporters of the opposition. The Popular Front pushed up to 100,000 people south across the Panj River to Afghanistan. Hundreds, if not thousands, died in crossing. International human rights organizations have gathered substantial evidence that after seizing control, the Popular Front and its Hisori allies carried out summary executions of Badakhshonis and Garmis.

The war's toll was enormous. Between 30,000 and 50,000 people died. Aside from the 100,000 who fled to Afghanistan, there were over 600,000 displaced persons in Tajikistan at the war's end. At least 200,000 more fled to other republics of the former Soviet Union, mostly to Russia, although statistics are incomplete and also reflect ethnic Russian migration that was likely to occur in any case. Qurghonteppe was severely depopulated and, according to one count, 35,000 dwellings in the region were destroyed.

The Opposition after the War

Opposition movements have established small bases of military operations in northern Afghanistan since the beginning of 1993. Estimated by foreign observers in Tajikistan to be about 5,000 men under arms, the forces are composed mostly of Tajik refugees who were forced to flee to Afghanistan during the war. The government in Dushanbe and their Russian military allies claim that Afghan *mujahedeen* (Islamic resistance fighters) have participated as mercenaries in some of the opposition's actions.

The forces are grouped together as the Islamic Resistance Movement; the most important commanders are drawn from the IRP, with the DP remaining as a junior partner. The Islamic nature of the opposition has grown during the fighters' and refugees' stay in Afghanistan, in part because they depend on sympathetic Muslim sponsors for their limited material support. Nonetheless, opposition leaders stress that they support the gradual, nonviolent introduction of Islamic values in Tajikistan and state that their fighters are motivated by a desire to return to their homeland, not religious fervor.

These lightly armed forces are no match for the current government, which is backed by Uzbekistani and Russian arms. Helped by mountainous terrain, the opposition conducts guerrilla attacks on the border and occasionally deep within the republic to remind the government and its allies in Tashkent and Moscow of its presence. Although clashes along the border occur almost daily, there have been no large-scale confrontations since July 1993.

In addition to the opposition in Afghanistan, some Tajik politicians and intellectuals have also formed the Coordinating Center of Democratic Forces of Tajikistan in Moscow to promote the opposition's cause by political means. The center was originally created in order to provide Moscow with a "constructive" opposition with which it could negotiate, although it has maintained unity with the forces in Afghanistan and speaks on their behalf. The Tajik opposition chose Moscow because it not unreasonably believed that Russia's own position would determine the situation. Since the beginning of this year, the center has begun talks with representatives of the government in Dushanbe.

The Current Government

Formed by the Supreme Soviet at the height of the civil war in November 1992, the current government reflects the military ascendancy of the Kulobi forces combined with the traditional domination of government administration by the Leninabadis. As commander of the Kulobi-dominated Popular Front, Sangak Safarov engineered the election of Emomali Rakhmonov, a former state farm director and a native of his village, as chairman of the Supreme Soviet. Kulobis also were appointed to head up the police and security agencies, and Popular Front units were loosely incorporated into these structures. The Kulobi preponderance at the top levels of government was later strengthened when Supreme Soviet Chairman Rakhmonov appointed Abdumajid Dostiev, a Kulobi leader who had fought in the Qurghonteppe region, as first deputy chairman in July 1993. Dostiev is in charge of many of the day-to-day functions and commands particular authority in the police and security forces.

Leninabadis generally head government agencies that are responsible for administering the economy. The first post-war prime minister, Abdumalik Abdullojonov, and his recent replacement, Abdujalil Samadov, are Leninabadis. Leninabadis also head the economic planning committee and Foreign Trade and Foreign Affairs ministries.

The Ministry of Defense is headed by Alexander Shishlyannikov, an ethnic Russian who had never lived in Tajikistan but had previously served in Soviet forces stationed in Uzbekistan. It is widely reputed that Shishlyannikov's appointment was due to heavy pressure from Uzbekistan's President Islam Karimov. Since taking office in January 1993, Shishlyannikov has been charged with creating republican armed forces with Russian assistance; these forces are to number 30,000 by the year 2000.

Over the course of 1993, friction grew between the Kulobi and Leninabadi groupings in the government and particularly their leaders, with Rakhmonov and Dostiev opposing Abdullojonov. The Kulobis' unprecedented level of control over the government as well as evidence that they were seizing lucrative positions in the republic did not sit well with the Leninabadis. On the other hand, Abdullojonov's clear ambitions and the fact that Leninabad Oblast's local government was pursuing autonomy riled the Kulobis. The conflict came to a head in late December 1993 when Prime Minister Abdullojonov was forced to resign and the central government succeeded in replacing several key local officials in Leninabad Oblast. Although Abdullojonov's replacement, Samadov, is also a Leninabadi, he is less attached to clan structures in Leninabad Oblast. He has a reputation as an experienced administrator (his background is in the republic's state planning committee) rather than a politician.

Another major figure in the republic's current political landscape is Safarali Kenjaev. Although Kenjaev played a major role in fighting the opposition—he was even wounded in the unsuccessful attack on Dushanbe—he was given no position in the new government. He was reportedly kept away from the November 1992 session of the Supreme Soviet in Khujand by Uzbekistani agents to ensure that he did not complicate the mathematics of the coalition between Kulobis and Leninabadis. By all accounts a very ambitious man, Kenjaev is unlikely to settle for his current official position as a state prosecutor in Leninabad Oblast. He still retains the loyalty of two sizable armed groups in the Hisor Valley as well as considerable support among the Leninabadis.

Foreign Involvement

Foreign entities were a major factor in the civil war, and they continue to have a decisive influence over events in Tajikistan. The main foreign players are: warlords in Afghanistan plus financial backers in the Islamic world; the government of Uzbekistan; and Russia, both through the 201st Motorized Infantry Division stationed in Dushanbe and the government in Moscow.

It is difficult to pinpoint when financial sources in the Islamic world and Afghan military groupings began to support the opposition. The present government asserts that the opposition received significant arms and financial support from Afghanistan during the civil war in 1992. The opposition denies this vigorously, stating that its forces had limited amounts of weaponry from local police arsenals. It is known that the opposition has received financial support from Pakistani and Arab sources since it set up camp in Afghanistan. However, at least part of this aid is humanitarian; it has been the only material support for tens of thousands of Tajik refugees who are stranded outside of areas in which international relief organizations operate. In addition, at least three different warlords in north central Afghanistan have reportedly provided training to the fighters. As noted above, the present government in Dushanbe claims that Afghan *mujahedeen* frequently join opposition fighters in their forays across the border.

Although Iran shares linguistic heritage with the Tajiks and reportedly was active during the conflict in 1992, it has since remained on the sidelines. For one thing, Sunni Tajiks from the IRP look to Pakistan and Saudi Arabia for support rather than to Shiite Iran. Also, Tehran is more interested in geopolitics than in exporting Islamic revolution to Central Asia. Iranian officials do not want to antagonize other governments in the region that take a dim view of radical Islam.

The foreign force most involved in the civil war was Uzbekistan. Tashkent sided heavily with the forces that brought the current government to power, providing the Popular Front with arms and training. Several eyewitness accounts, some from Russian journalists, claim that Uzbekistani Interior Ministry troops even participated in many of the military actions in the Qurghonteppe region and in the capture of Dushanbe, a charge Tashkent denies. Uzbekistani planes bombed villages in the Karategin Valley (the Garmi areas) in early 1993 and also Badakhshon in August 1993. Uzbekistan currently has numerous advisers to the present government stationed in Dushanbe and Leninabad Oblast, particularly in the police and security structures. Uzbekistan's leaders stress that they are helping their neighbor on the invitation of the legitimate host government and vigorously deny any wrongdoing.

Uzbekistan's active stance in Tajikistan is not surprising given the overlapping of Uzbeks and Tajiks along the countries' 720-mile-long border. As Tashkent notes, it is difficult to remain neutral when brutal fighting occurs next door and involves one's kin. In addition, President Karimov of Uzbekistan was and remains deeply concerned with the existence of political Islam and aggressively anti-*nomenklatura* movements in neighboring Tajikistan. President Karimov also was alarmed by the elements of Tajik nationalism in the opposition; Tajik oppositionists assert that Karimov sided with the Popular Front simply to foment civil war in Tajikistan in order to weaken the country, thereby preempting any Tajik claims to Samarkand and Bukhara. Whatever the truth of these allegations, the installation of a government that draws on the old Leninabadi administrative elite and depends on Uzbekistani support suits Tashkent.

Uzbekistan's role as kingmaker in Tajikistan has been sharply curtailed since Russia's sudden reassertion of interest in the area in the summer of 1993. Until that point, Russia's position had been a disjointed combination of sporadic attention from Moscow and the presence of the 201st Motorized Infantry Division, a relic of the Soviet Army. The Russian government appeared less concerned about who won the war than about ensuring that Tajikistan stayed in its orbit. Growing concern over IRP links with Afghan groups plus anti-Russian statements by an opposition leader eventually tilted Moscow against the opposition groups.

The stance of the 201st during the civil war reflected confusion and lack of discipline in the ranks. Soldiers sold, gave, or surrendered weapons to the Popular Front but also sold arms to the opposition. Although some troops reportedly engaged in combat on the Popular Front's side, the 201st also defended Dushanbe over the autumn of 1992 from attacks by forces aligned against the opposition. The commander of the 201st joined a governing council formed in opposition-dominated Dushanbe in November 1992.

However, when the chips were down toward the end of the war, Russian troops stood aside to allow the Popular Front to seize Dushanbe in December 1992. After the Popular Front's victory, the 201st and Moscow became increasingly involved in supporting the current government. Most important, Russian troops have been thrust into the role of defending Tajikistan's border with Afghanistan against infiltration by the opposition.

Russia assumed a high-profile role in Tajikistan only after the opposition launched an attack on a border post that left 25 of its soldiers dead on July 13, 1993. Moscow moved with singular coordination and quickness to beef up its military presence and to involve the other Central Asian nations, except Turkmenistan, in guarding the Tajikistan-Afghanistan border. During the autumn of 1993, Russia put pressure on the current government to come to an accommodation with the opposition; although some of the political elements in the opposition are certainly not to Moscow's taste, Russia wants to avoid another Afghanistan.

Moscow has invested heavily in the republic in order to safeguard its interests by ensuring a measure of stability. In addition to some 24,000 troops and a commitment to help Tajikistan build up its own army, Russia has propped up the republic's economy by allowing it to remain in the rouble zone, albeit on conditions that greatly limit the republic's fiscal autonomy. Russia provided Tajikistan with a loan of 30 billion new Russian roubles in January 1994 (roughly $25 million at the time) and promised another 30 billion to keep the republic afloat. Officials in Dushanbe admit that Tajikistan has more or less protectorate status and must do Moscow's bidding on most issues.

Post-War Tajikistan

Once the large-scale hostilities were over, the present government's central effort in 1993 was to ensure that the country's refugees returned home, which in most cases meant back to the Qurghonteppe region. The majority of the 600,000 displaced persons within Tajikistan had returned by late spring 1993, on their own or as a result of government coercion. The International Committee of the Red Cross, the office of the United Nations High Commissioner for Refugees (UNHCR), and others scrambled to provide material support. UNHCR also facilitated the return of over 30,000 refugees from Afghanistan.

As of late January 1994, there were officially only 25,000 displaced persons left in Tajikistan. At least another 30,000 refugees remain in parts of Afghanistan where UNHCR is unable to operate; Human Rights Watch/Helsinki Watch has published evidence that forces in Afghanistan and opposition leaders are coercing these persons to remain and support the fight against the regime in Dushanbe.

International aid officials as well as human rights groups note that the returnees, most of whom were Garmis, frequently encountered hostility from the local police and remaining population, who were generally Kulobis and Uzbeks. There were numerous property seizures, and returnees were even killed. Fortunately, incidents declined dramatically as summer 1993 progressed.

While it has achieved relative success in returning the refugees, the central government faces a far greater challenge in building a sense of nationhood in Tajikistan. Not surprisingly given the economic devastation wrought by the conflict and the country's fierce regionalism, the government in Dushanbe is able to exercise only limited control over much of the country.

Leninabad Oblast and Badakhshon are virtually self-governing. The former, geographically and economically isolated from the rest of the country, hardly paid any taxes to the central government in 1993 and asserted autonomous control over its local police and security forces. At one point in late 1992, its local leaders were openly considering seceding to Uzbekistan. For its part, Badakhshon's leadership has declared the region an independent republic, although it agreed to suspend this decision in return for an unwritten promise from Dushanbe that the central government would not bring its conflict with the opposition into the region. While not openly supportive of the opposition, Badakhshon's leadership allows opposition fighters to move freely as long as they do not cause problems for the local government. Reliant on imports of food and consumer items, Badakhshon does not enjoy the economic autonomy of Leninabad Oblast. However, the region is fiercely independent of Dushanbe and looks more to far-off—and hence more neutral—Russia for economic support.

The government faces great difficulties in enforcing basic law and order in many areas. The civil war left a tremendous number of arms in the hands of the population. In addition, the Kulobi armed units fell apart when Sangak Safarov died in a mysterious shoot-out with one of his lieutenants in March 1993. Although the government officially disbanded the Popular Front and tried to absorb some of its supporters into state structures, many have kept their weapons and their independence. There are numerous reports of deadly turf fights among these and other armed groups. The government has been unable and, according to its detractors, unwilling to punish many criminals or enforce its demands for the surrender of weapons.

While it called for national reconciliation and announced some partial amnesties, Tajikistan's present government vigorously suppressed any vestiges of support for the opposition. Human rights groups have criticized the government for the detention of prisoners without trial, heavy media censorship and intimidation of journalists, and ambivalence about violence committed by former Popular Front fighters against alleged supporters of the opposition. Opposition leaders were tried and condemned for treason in absentia, and the country's Supreme Court formally banned the four main opposition movements on June 21, 1993. Despite public gestures in spring 1994 to repair the government's image abroad, reports of harassment of suspected opposition supporters continue.

Under pressure from its Russian benefactors as well as calls from the United Nations and others in the international community to reach a peaceful settlement, the current government began in late 1993 to consider talks with the opposition. Members of the

Dushanbe government began quietly to seek meetings with leaders of the Coordinating Center in Moscow. The two sides agreed to hold talks on March 16, 1994, but they were postponed when the Dushanbe government's chief negotiator was killed. Talks finally got under way in early April between a modest delegation from Dushanbe, led by the minister responsible for handling refugees and the chairman of the Coordinating Center. On April 21 they agreed to repatriate refugees from Afghanistan, and in June they held further talks in Iran, which ended in a stalemate.

Within the country the government has ambitious plans to hold a popular referendum in September 1994 on presidential elections and a draft constitution adopted by Parliament in July. The government asserts that these changes are needed to confirm Tajikistan's new independent status. However, given the lawlessness in Tajikistan, the repressiveness of the government, and the fact that many refugees remain outside the republic, the elections will probably have little legitimacy.

The election of a new head of state is likely to stir antagonism between the Leninabadi and Kulobi groupings as they jockey for power. The existing legal parties in Tajikistan have strong regional affiliations with either Kulob or Leninabad. The only two candidates who have declared themselves are Rakhmonov and Abdullojonov, personal and clan adversaries. Some of Leninabad Oblast's more ambitious leaders previously advocated government reform, specifically the institution of a presidency, to recapture preeminence in the central government from the militarily stronger Kulobi grouping. The Leninabadi elite is counting on the votes of the oblast's population of 1.5 million along with the likely support of the country's 1 million-strong Uzbek population.

The dominant Kulobi faction appears to have little to gain. Kulobis' natural allies are other historically disadvantaged southerners; there have been reports of Kulobis making overtures to returning Garmis and Badakhshonis in Qurghonteppe in the face of Uzbeks' increased power in the region. However, rapprochement will be difficult after the recent bloodshed between the groups.

ECONOMICS

Material Assets Profile

Tajikistan is less fortunate than its Central Asian neighbors in terms of mineral wealth, although it contains deposits of valuable metals. Like the Kyrgyz Republic, mountainous Tajikistan must import virtually all of its gas and oil but hopes to offset the lack of fossil fuels with the large potential for hydroelectric power. However, although the republic is home to dams such as the Nurek—one of the world's highest—additional investment is needed to develop this sector.

The country, particularly outside Leninabad Oblast, is largely agricultural. Soviet planners developed the Vakhsh Valley of the Qurghonteppe region into a center of cotton production; before the civil war, more than half of the republic's cotton crop came from this area. According to official statistics, Tajikistan produced 524,000 tons of cotton in 1993, a nearly 20 percent increase from 1992 when fighting disrupted production, but still far below prewar levels. In addition to cotton, the republic's most important agricultural products are fruits (especially lemons) and vegetables. The republic has traditionally relied on imports of wheat and rice.

The agricultural sector was extremely hard hit by the civil war. Qurghonteppe suffered destruction of property and depopulation. The cotton crop in 1993 was sown and reaped almost entirely by hand, as machinery and fuel were unavailable.

The republic has a small industrial base, although it boasts a uranium processing facility (which cannot produce weapons-grade nuclear fuel) as well as an aluminum plant. There are also some textile plants in Leninabad Oblast. However, Tajikistan relies for the most part on imports for industrial goods.

The country's spectacular and largely untouched countryside, particularly in Badakhshon, lends itself to tourism and hunting. A great deal of investment is required to develop this industry, though adventurous individuals from the West have begun to visit the republic, mostly to go hunting.

Performance in 1993

Although better than the previous year, 1993 was very tough on the population in Tajikistan, especially outside Leninabad Oblast. According to official statistics, GDP fell by about 20 percent while the consumer price index jumped by over 6000 percent. In Dushanbe, lines for bread begin to form outside the city's one bakery at 5:00 A.M.: fuel shortages make deliveries to city outlets a rare occurrence and, although there is no threat of starvation, bread can be scarce. Apartments were very cold over the winter owing to the lack of fuel supplies for central heating. Bazaars have food, but at prices higher than in Moscow, although salaries are a fraction of Russian ones. State stores are mostly empty.

Russian and, to a lesser extent, Uzbekistani credits to purchase key agricultural products were crucial to sustaining the republic's economy. Foreign observers estimate that Moscow funded more than two-thirds of Tajikistan's budget. Other, non-CIS countries supplied humanitarian assistance, including more than $14 million-worth of grain from the United States in 1993.

Tajikistan is the only former Soviet republic to join the new rouble zone, which allows it to tap into Russia's relative economic strength. The decision of Uzbekistan and others to abandon the old Soviet rouble in mid-November 1993 hit the republic hard: excess old roubles flooded into Tajikistan's already depleted market, causing an enormous jump in the consumer price index (more than 200 percent) in the last two months of 1993. Recognizing that Tajikistan was in no shape to introduce its own currency, Russia signed a general agreement to provide 120 billion 1993-issue Russian roubles (about $100 million at the time) in November 1993 and delivered its first allotment of 30 billion roubles to Tajikistan, allowing it to make the transition from old Soviet-era roubles to the new ones in January 1994. However, this has been a mixed blessing, since strict limits were placed on the amount that could be transferred. New roubles remain in very short supply.

The chaos of civil war and its aftermath have precluded serious efforts to reform the economy or develop legislation to undergird private enterprise, although the current government has professed a commitment to the market. Enterprises and land nominally remain state-owned, but there are numerous reports of armed groups seizing property. The government wants to stabilize the situation before it considers serious reforms.

Non-CIS Involvement

Owing to the instability, there has been minimal foreign economic interest in Tajikistan. In addition, with the exception of some metals and cotton, the republic has few goods of immediate interest to foreign investors. The largest foreign involvement thus far consists of a jeans factory built in Khujand by a Hong Kong–based company.

FOREIGN RELATIONS

For obvious reasons, Tajikistan's foreign relations are focused on its two main benefactors, Russia and Uzbekistan, and its policy toward others keeps in step with theirs. The most interesting development in the country's non-CIS relations has been the Dushanbe government's pursuit of good relations with ethnic Tajik Prime Minister Berhanuddin Rabbani of Afghanistan; in 1993 the two countries exchanged official visits of heads of state. Both sides have agreed not to interfere in each other's affairs, although this has little practical effect since Rabbani and his ally, Afghanistan's defense minister Ahmed Shah Massoud, do not control the territory on which the Tajikistani opposition is based and Dushanbe has no influence over factions opposed to Rabbani in Afghanistan.

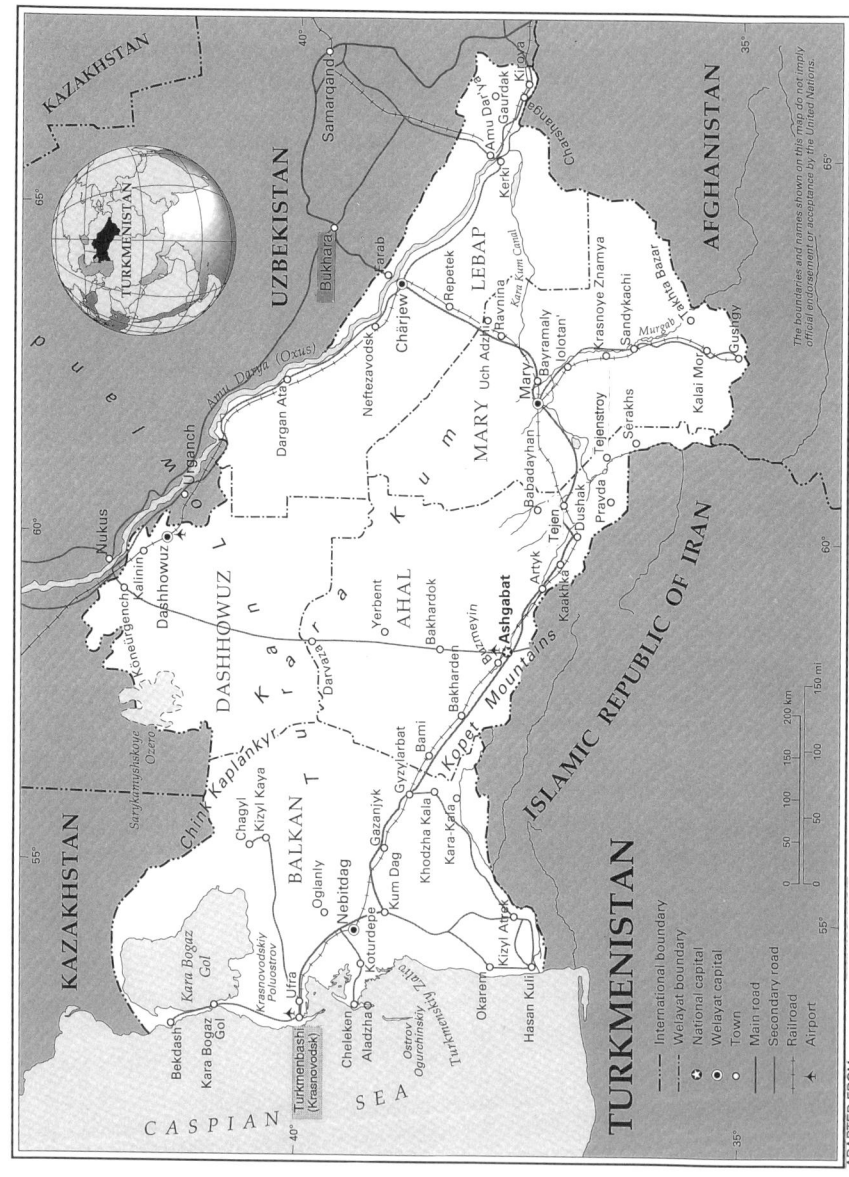

TURKMENISTAN

POLITICS

President Saparmurat Niyazov

A lack of major ethnic or regional clan divisions within the body politic and a relatively stable economy with bright prospects for the future distinguish Turkmenistan from other Central Asian countries. The titular nationality, the Turkmens (sometimes referred to as Turcomans), are overwhelmingly rural, which breeds political conservatism and a disinclination toward politics. Moreover Turkmenistan, with less than 4 million people, is home to some of the world's largest natural gas reserves.

These happy circumstances have allowed President Saparmurat Niyazov to dominate local politics to a degree not matched by any other leader in the former Soviet Union. A referendum held on January 15, 1994, confirmed Niyazov by a 99 percent margin as president until the year 2000. Niyazov has taken advantage of the republic's stabilizing characteristics to indulge in a campaign of self-glorification as the country's father or, as he is officially known, *Turkmenbashi* (Head of the Turkmens).

State officials outdo one another in their praise of Niyazov. The president's likeness appears everywhere, including on the bills of the country's new currency and on special gold commemorative coins. His name has been attached to schools, factories, roads, an army regiment, and even the Kara Kum Canal, replacing Lenin's. The republic's second largest city, a gas town and port founded and inhabited mostly by Russians, has been renamed Turkmenbashi. In November 1993, Ashgabat's newspapers began to carry articles from institutions all over the country supporting *Turkmenbashi*'s candidacy for the Nobel Peace Prize; it was supposedly first put forward in a statement signed by literary figures from elsewhere in the former Soviet Union, but these writers later claimed that this was a fabrication.

President Niyazov's greatest source of power lies in the development of the country's natural gas reserves. For the foreseeable future, the government will maintain strict control over the republic's natural assets, including the determination of who receives a share of the resultant wealth. Although Turkmenistan's overall living standards have not skyrocketed since the republic assumed control of its gas extraction, a new class of persons benefiting from it financially is taking shape. In addition to sponsoring a rich elite, President Niyazov has adopted several measures to win support from the populace. Promising to turn the country into a "second Kuwait," the Niyazov government has imitated Gulf-style social benefits, including free heating, electricity, and water since 1993 and heavily subsidized bread beginning in 1994.

President Niyazov also has a strong power base in the former Communist Party, now renamed the Turkmenistan Democratic Party (TDP), which is the only legal organized political movement in the country. Niyazov became the first secretary of the Communist Party of Turkmenistan back in 1985, making him the longest-serving head of a republican Communist structure in Central Asia when independence arrived. Although he has created networks of personal loyalty in the government rather than relying on the party hierarchy, Niyazov continues to benefit from a base of support among administrative personnel who were members of the Communist Party. In recognition of this force, Niyazov signed a decree that automatically conferred membership in the TDP to members of the former Communist Party.

President Niyazov also draws on clan relationships among the Turkmen people. The Turkmens have preserved their historical tribal roots better than other Central Asian states and culturally were among the least touched by the Soviet state. Niyazov is from the country's dominant *Teke* clan, although he himself is an orphan. By granting various clans a role in government administration or a share of Turkmenistan's wealth, he has given them a stake in the current regime and an incentive to secure other members' loyalty.

In addition to fashioning a tribal leader's image for Niyazov, the government has created structures that combine traditional consensus-based Turkmen tribal decision-making practices with firm governmental control. President Niyazov regularly consults with Turkmen *aksakals* (elders) on major state decisions. Turkmenistan instituted a supreme consultative body, the *Halk Maslahati* (People's Council), composed of the president and government officials as well as specially elected representatives from local districts, the country's parliament, and the judiciary. The body is supposed to decide on crucial issues of state, such as the declaration of war and ratification of treaties, and provide consultation for President Niyazov in the spirit of consensus politics. Since most of the members of this body are Niyazov appointees, they exhibit a striking degree of agreement on his policies.

Political Opposition

The Turkmen leader's acts of largesse and promises of leading the country to prosperity reduce any base of public unhappiness upon which an opposition could draw. However, there are some among the republic's small urban population who disagree with President Niyazov's style of rule. Furthermore, there is a potential pool of discontent as most of the population has yet to feel the benefits of Turkmenistan's gas earnings.

The government has not allowed opposition groups to develop. Small groupings such as the *Agzybirlik* (Unity), a Turkmen nationalist movement of a few hundred active members which arose in 1989, and the Democratic Party, a small gathering mostly of intellectuals (not to be confused with the renamed Communist Party), have not been allowed to register as political movements. Perhaps the most serious threat comes from the country's first post-independence foreign minister, Abdy Kuliev, who broke with President Niyazov and moved to Moscow to establish himself in opposition. However, none of these players commands an organization of any size or significance.

The opposition has accused the government of intimidation through threats of violence, detention without trial, dismissal from work, and the application of similar tactics on family members. Human rights organizations have also criticized the government for its suppression of political opponents as well as its heavy-handed censorship of the media. Oppositionists have been forced either to make peace with the Niyazov government or to emigrate. Like other authoritarian leaders in Central Asia, Niyazov cites the need for stability in republics of the former Soviet Union as justification for the harsh measures used to put down opposition.

Interethnic Relations

Turkmenistan has arguably the most harmonious interethnic relations in all of Central Asia. The country's two largest ethnic minorities are the Russians and the Uzbeks, each of which makes up about 9 percent of the population. Although Russians are concerned about the promotion of the Turkmen language and ethnic Turkmen in government as well as Niyazov's personality cult, the country's economic potential and comparative stability reduce their anxiety. Some of the relatively few Russians who left in 1990 and 1991 have even returned.

ethnic breakdown
Turkmen, 73.3 %
Russian, 9.8 %
Uzbek, 9.0%
Other, 5.9%
Kazakh, 2.0%

Turkmenistani authorities recognize that they have a stake in good ethnic relations, since the Russians provide the skilled labor for the country's extractive industries. Ashgabat has enacted several measures aimed at allaying Russian concerns, such as providing dual citizenship and material guarantees for Russians who wish to emigrate from Turkmenistan, as well as for Russians serving in the armed forces inherited from the Soviet Union. In addition, relatively trouble-free relations with Russia have kept ethnic tensions at a minimum.

Similarly, there is little discontent in the Uzbek community that makes up a large proportion of the towns along the Amu Darya basin in Turkmenistan's northeast. The only friction comes from the rather limited resentment among Turkmens of the fact that Uzbeks tend to dominate the produce markets in the towns (similar to the situation in the southern part of the Kyrgyz Republic). Uzbeks participate in local political structures and receive Uzbek language textbooks and schooling through a bilateral agreement with Uzbekistan.

Islam

The Turkmens are among the most devoutly Muslim of the peoples of the former Soviet Union, having adopted Islam to a far greater extent than the similarly pastoral Kazakhs or Kyrgyz farther east. Furthermore, Islam remained relatively untouched by the Soviet presence, since religion among the nomadic Turkmens relied far less on a structured, rooted clergy than it did among the Uzbeks and Tajiks. By the same token, Islam is not a politically organizing force in Turkmenistan.

As part of the general emphasis on Turkmen cultural renewal, President Niyazov has encouraged the growth of Islam. The state recognizes Muslim holidays and sponsors mosque construction and the dissemination of Islamic literature. Although a member of the Communist Party for nearly 30 years, Niyazov stresses his own devotion, and even erected a monument commemorating his hajj to Mecca on a square in Ashgabat. At the same time, he has vigorously spoken against mixing Islam with politics.

ECONOMICS

Material Assets Profile

Turkmenistan is the fourth largest producer of natural gas in the world, after the United States, Russia, and Canada. It has proven and probable reserves of up to 1.3 trillion cubic meters, with almost as much in possible reserves. In addition to gas, Turkmenistan has significant oil deposits (over 1 billion metric tons). It is a major exporter of both, mostly to other CIS countries.

Geography and infrastructure force Turkmenistan to depend on the old Soviet pipeline system to export its mineral wealth. The country's natural gas continues to be channeled mainly to other former Soviet republics; in 1992 only 16 percent of exports went to non-CIS countries. Unfortunately, the Caucasus republics and Ukraine and, to a lesser extent, Kazakhstan and Uzbekistan are chronically in arrears; by mid-February 1994, Ashgabat asserted that CIS countries owed Turkmenistan about $1.5 billion in back payments, half of which was due from Ukraine. Turkmenistan cut off gas deliveries to Ukraine for a few days in late February 1994 until Kiev paid up.

Turning off the tap is not a solution, since the pipeline system prevents Turkmenistan from reallocating supplies to other destinations. Turkmenistan's natural gas flows through pipelines to Russia, where it is pooled with that country's natural gas and then distributed among the republics of the former Soviet Union and to European consumers. With a financial stake in exporting its own gas, Russia is loath to increase Turkmenistan's quota flowing through the pipelines to Europe. There is no public friction between Turkmenistan and Russia on the issue, but it leaves Ashgabat with little room to maneuver.

The republic has very little industry aside from oil and gas extraction; only about 10 percent of the labor force is industrial. There is some light industry for processing agricultural goods, such as cotton fiber. Turkmenistan's extremely low level of industrialization, particularly in manufacturing, has meant that it has suffered relatively little from the breakup of the USSR.

Much of the population and the majority of ethnic Turkmens work in agriculture. Since Turkmenistan is mainly desert, cultivation is limited to areas along the Amu Darya and the Kara Kum Canal, a 700-mile-long channel that stretches from the Amu across the republic. The main crop is long-fiber cotton, but some vegetables and fruits are also grown. As in Uzbekistan, the country is trying to shift its agriculture away from the emphasis on cotton imposed by planners in Moscow; the country made an important advance when it became self-sufficient in rice production in 1993. Nonetheless, Turkmenistan relies on imports of several foodstuffs. Animal husbandry, mainly of sheep, horses, and cattle, is a traditional economic activity of the historically nomadic Turkmens. Today it accounts for about a quarter of agricultural production.

Despite its wealth in natural resources, Turkmenistan suffers from underdevelopment; Soviet planners were far more concerned with extracting the republic's gas and transporting it to Europe than with improving living standards for the local population. Many villages continue to be without running water or, ironically, reliable supplies of fuel.

Performance in 1993

Unlike the rest of Central Asia, Turkmenistan's economic performance during 1993 showed improvement over 1992 in both the agricultural and industrial sectors. GDP was up by nearly 8 percent. The all-important indicator of natural gas production was up by 9 percent, at 65.2 billion metric tons, although this figure is still lower than the 80.4 billion metric tons produced in 1991. However, while these indicators suggest a robust economy (even taking into consideration the uncertainties of statistics from the former Soviet Union), the standard of living for the population fell during 1993. Even though utilities were free, the consumer price index outstripped income at rates of over 2 to 1 for the first ten months of the year.

On November 1, 1993, the country took an important step toward taking control of its economy by introducing its own currency, the *manat*. Foreseeing the eventual demise of the rouble zone, the Niyazov government planned the measure well in advance. Nonetheless, the transition has not been easy. In order to keep the money supply down, the government delayed payment of some wages and stipends and put limitations on the amount of old roubles that could be converted freely. A cash shortage was evident even a month after the supposed introduction. Concurrent with the *manat*'s introduction, the state cut back on price subsidies, severely reducing the population's buying power.

The government has since opted to print more money with less backing in hard currency reserves, undermining confidence in the *manat*. Although the official rate has remained 2 *manats* to the dollar, it was already 8 to 1 to the U.S. dollar on the black market in early December and had reportedly jumped to 35 to 40 to the dollar by the end of January. Despite these economic problems, Turkmenistan has the wherewithal to achieve macroeconomic stabilization in the not too distant future.

Aside from the currency reforms and easing of some price subsidies, President Niyazov's government has been reluctant to implement market-oriented measures. In his outline for developing Turkmenistan, "Ten Years of Prosperity," Niyazov emphasizes the need to avoid socially destabilizing measures. As part of this strategy, there has been no move to privatize the two key areas of the country's economy: the agricultural sector (land) and the gas and oil industry. Even many small retail shops remain state-owned. The state plans to continue subsidizing utilities and bread, and has reportedly promised to provide each family with a house and car.

Non-CIS Involvement

Turkmenistan's fabulous natural wealth and its relative stability are obvious draws for foreign companies. The Niyazov government counts on foreign investment to exploit its gas and oil. As of the end of 1993, the biggest deal with a non-CIS partner in the gas industry was a joint venture with Argentina-based Berdidas to exploit two fields. Turkish, Arab, Dutch, and American companies have also signed deals to develop the country's oil industry.

Outside of the extractive industries, firms from several Western nations, led by Italy, have invested in ventures to provide consumer goods to the republic's starved market. Out of more than 243 joint ventures registered by the end of 1993, the majority related to the country's retail sector. Turkey has also been signing agreements to develop the cotton industry. Finally, small-scale trade with Iran and Turkey is increasing rapidly.

FOREIGN RELATIONS

The Niyazov government pursues a policy of "positive neutrality," defined as seeking mutually beneficial bilateral relations with all countries while eschewing supranational structures that exert any kind of control over Turkmenistan's internal affairs or policies. The republic is only an associate member of the CIS and looks upon the body as a purely consultative structure. President Niyazov participates in the meetings of Central Asian leaders, but has studiously avoided entering into any kind of regional bloc. Turkmenistan's independent stance was highlighted when it alone among the Central Asian states refused to contribute troops to a Russia-led CIS initiative to reinforce the Tajikistan-Afghanistan border in August 1993. President Niyazov argued that Turkmenistan would absolutely not intervene in any other country.

One need not look far to find the rationale for Turkmenistan's emphasis on independence. Because of the lack of industry aside from natural resource extraction, Turkmenistan has much less need for close coordination of economic policies within the CIS. More important, the republic's leadership is suspicious of anything smacking of a "center" that would siphon off its natural gas earnings to support less fortunate regions or a ruling caste in Moscow. After all, it was due to Moscow's planning that energy-rich Turkmenistan remained one of the poorest and least developed of the Soviet republics.

While keeping the CIS at arm's length, Turkmenistan has sought close bilateral relations with Russia. President Niyazov recognizes that Russia effectively controls the republic's wealth because the current pipeline system gives it a monopoly over Turkmenistan's gas exports. Reports that Moscow withheld the desert republic's earnings from gas exports in December 1993 only confirm these circumstances.

Niyazov has addressed the concerns of Russia's leadership. Turkmenistan broke with all the other former Soviet republics in agreeing to institute dual citizenship with Russia; President Boris Yeltsin of Russia became the first dual citizen when the agreement was signed on December 24, 1993. The two republics have also signed a series of agreements on the transfer of Soviet Army units along the Iranian border to Turkmenistan's control, with numerous guarantees for Russian control over air defense systems. President Niyazov has also reassured Russia that it will have a leading role in the development of Turkmenistan's oil and gas industry.

Uzbekistan is also a priority for Turkmenistan. The two countries have regulated key issues binding them: the needs of the ethnic Uzbek minority in Turkmenistan, deliveries of natural gas to Uzbekistan's western regions, and utilization of the waters of the Amu Darya river, which runs along the border. The last issue will be a source of increasing concern, since both countries face growing environmental problems owing to pollution and misuse of water.

Despite its intimacy with a Russia often jealous of foreign influences, Ashgabat has been consistently supportive of a special relationship with Turkey. Closer both linguistically and geographically to Turkey than other Central Asian states, Turkmenistan has taken greater advantage of the cultural exchange programs Ankara has offered. It was the first of the Central Asian turcophone states to adopt the Latin alphabet and has moved farther than any other in switching over to the new script. Turkish business entities reportedly receive extra privileges in Turkmenistan, and trade between the two countries is brisk.

Turkmenistan has established working ties with Iran. Well over a million ethnic Turkmen inhabit the immediate regions across the Iranian border, and Iran and Turkmenistan have signed an agreement to allow the populations in their respective border areas to visit one another six times per year without visa requirements. However, Ashgabat is concerned about the infiltration of radical Islamic politics from the south, and visa regulations are stricter for most Iranians than for Westerners. Also, Iran is the logical alternative to Russia as a conduit for exports, and there are plans to build a pipeline to Iran's seaports and to connect the countries' railroads. Both nations have a deep interest in developing this infrastructure, but they are hamstrung by lack of capital.

Relations with the West have been clouded by criticism of the Niyazov government's human rights record. On at least two occasions, the government has locked up oppositionists in advance of visits by U.S. government officials, causing a good deal of friction. Although U.S. presidents have met with Akaev and Nazarbaev, Clinton did not meet with Niyazov when the latter visited the United States in 1993. Nonetheless, Western business interests in the area are likely to grow.

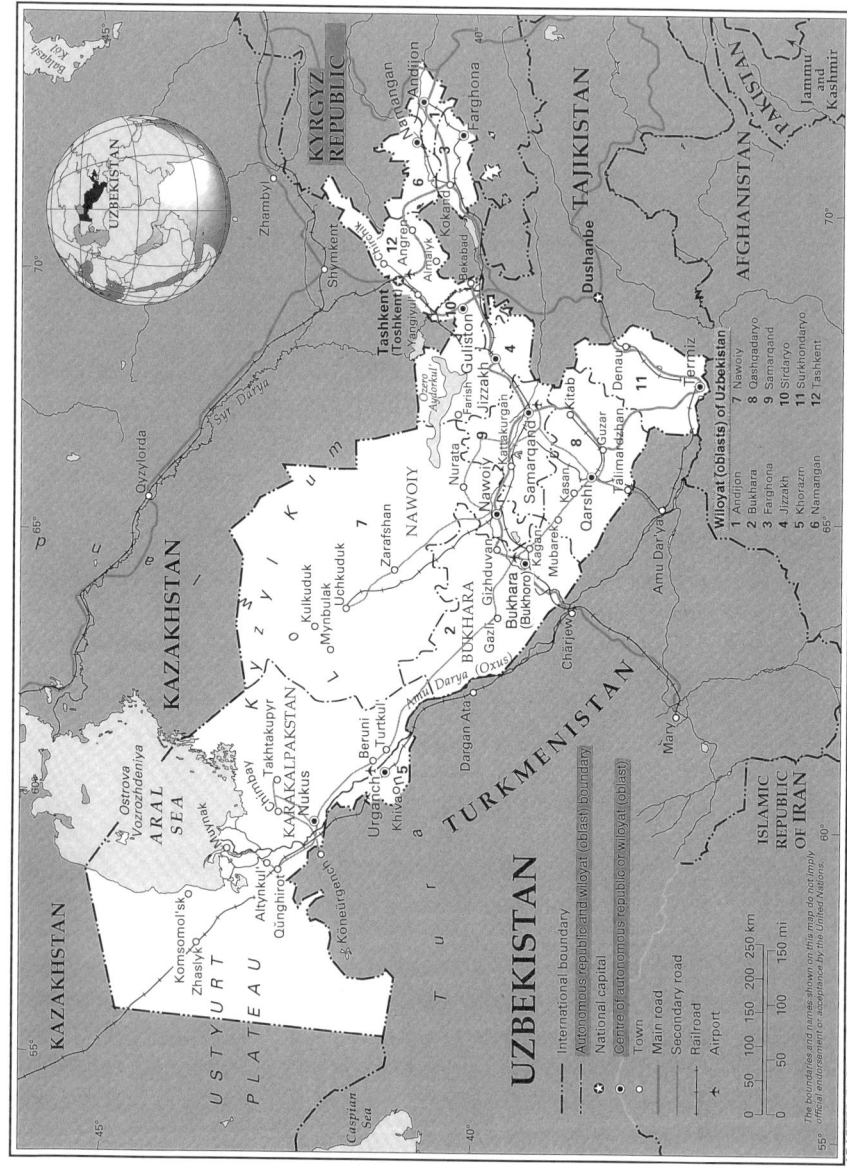

UZBEKISTAN

POLITICS

President Islam Karimov

As in neighboring Turkmenistan and Kazakhstan, Uzbekistan's politics are largely a one-man show. President Islam Karimov has managed to concentrate political decision-making in his own hands while neutralizing if not eliminating potential rivals. Presidential decrees have the force of law, and 96 percent of the legislature is composed of members of Karimov's People's Democratic Party (PDP), the successor to the Communist Party. At present the only credible threat to Karimov's control over the republic's affairs are the economic woes that Uzbekistan, like all the former Soviet republics, is experiencing. Uzbekistani officials often note that stability provided by the centralization of power is necessary for the short term to overcome the economic crisis.

Born in Samarkand in 1939, Karimov spent most of his career working in the republic's State Planning Committee (*Gosplan*), finally becoming the committee's chairman in 1986. As an orphan brought up by the Soviet state, he did not have strong connections to the powerful clans that, together with Moscow, determined politics in Uzbekistan. His rise within the political leadership of the Communist Party hierarchy in Uzbekistan became possible only after a huge corruption scandal over cotton earnings had discredited the old party elite in the mid-1980s. The Gorbachev government in Moscow allowed the scandal to become public to undermine the corrupt, nepotistic bosses of the Communist Party who opposed reforms.

Karimov's lack of clan ties plus his background in administration rather than the party hierarchy worked in his favor as the Gorbachev-led Communist Party sought new faces in Uzbekistan. With support from Moscow, Karimov became first secretary of the Communist Party cell of the small Kashkadarya Oblast in December 1986, clearly in preparation for the jump he took to first secretary of the Uzbek Communist Party in June 1989. He spent a few years consolidating his hold over the party apparatus, which was staffed with many persons associated with the old elite. Not surprisingly, this period (roughly from the end of 1989 to mid-1991) corresponded to the rise of independent political groupings, which Karimov moved to neutralize once he was confident of his power base.

Karimov claims popular legitimacy from his victory in presidential elections in December 1991 against an opposition candidate by a margin of eight to one. Although many in the political opposition have claimed that the vote was rigged, most observers conceded that, even if there were irregularities, Karimov was a lock to win because of traditional respect for incumbent power in the republic's rural areas.

Although the PDP is very much the president's party (it sponsored Karimov's candidacy), it does not wield significant influence. Karimov has gradually bypassed party structures, shifting power to government agencies headed by personal allies and his own presidential staff. These individuals' loyalty rests on Karimov's patronage. At the same time, persons with too many ties to the traditionally powerful clans or the old Communist Party elite have been weeded out of government.

The Karimov government has aggressively put down opposition. Human rights groups have documented numerous cases of physical intimidation of opposition figures, imprisonment without trial, and heavy censorship of the media. Uzbekistan's leadership asserts that its harshness toward a few troublemakers is warranted for overall stability during the country's infancy, pointing to the civil conflict in Tajikistan as an example of what happens if events spin out of control.

Uzbekistan's leadership has been perhaps the most active in Central Asia in promoting public holidays and cultural events to build a sense of nationhood. The government also stresses continuity between modern Uzbekistan and the region's rich heritage, paying much public reverence to Timur (Tamerlane), Ulug Beg, Ibn Sind (Avicenna), Al-Biruni, and other famous medieval leaders and scholars who lived in what is now Uzbekistan (much to the irritation of other Central Asian peoples, who see this as Uzbek appropriation of history; in particular, the Tajiks claim Ibn Sind and Al-Biruni as their forefathers).

Opposition Parties

The two most publicized opposition groups in Uzbekistan are the umbrella movement *Birlik* (Unity) and the party *Erk* (Will). At the peak of its influence in 1989, *Birlik* was the strongest independent political movement in Central Asia, capable of organizing demonstrations of tens of thousands on the streets of Tashkent. It pursued an agenda of further democratization of Communist-dominated politics and the revival of Uzbek culture, including the designation of Uzbek as the state language. *Erk* was mostly composed of intellectuals who broke with *Birlik* because of personal clashes and differences over how much to cooperate with the Karimov government.

Both groups have been neutralized. Under intense pressure from the government since 1991, members and supporters of *Birlik* and *Erk* have not been permitted to organize in Uzbekistan. The two groups were effectively banned in 1993, when the government refused to register them as political parties, ostensibly on the grounds that they had too few members to qualify. With one exception, their leadership is in exile in Russia, Turkey, or the United States. In addition to government pressure, or perhaps as a result of it, the groups have also been hampered by frequent internal divisions.

The Karimov government has also undercut *Birlik*'s and *Erk*'s attractiveness by manipulating the groups' platforms. On the one hand, Karimov appropriated some of the opposition's goals when he declared Uzbekistan's independence and sponsored a constitution making Uzbek the state language, though he did this only when the Soviet Union's demise was a foregone conclusion after the failed putsch in August 1991. At the same time, Karimov exploited statements by the opposition and fears of ethnic violence among Uzbekistan's population, especially in the Russian community, to discredit *Birlik* and *Erk* as radical Uzbek nationalist organizations. Although members of both *Birlik* and *Erk* vigorously deny this characterization and point to their collaboration with ethnic Russians and others, this perception has taken hold in the population. At the same time, Karimov presents himself as a bulwark for interethnic harmony in the republic in contrast to these "nationalists."

Several other less prominent movements that arose during the political ferment of 1989 to 1991 have curtailed their activities if not dissolved completely for a variety of reasons, not the least of which was harassment by the authorities. These groups include a Tajik cultural rights group, "Samarkand," and a pan-Turkic organization, "Turkestan." Islamic groups have mostly gone underground, and it is difficult to estimate their real strength.

There are two legal parties other than President Karimov's PDP: the *Vattan Tarraqoti* (Fatherland and Progress) Party (FPP) and the *Istiklol Iuli* (Path of Independence) Party (PIP). While its programmatic statements have called for slightly quicker market reforms, the FPP is avowedly pro-Karimov. Until January 1994, the party was headed by Usmon Azimov, formerly a close aide to Karimov. The PIP was founded in early 1994 by Shodi Karimov, a professor of Uzbek history who had been a member of *Birlik* and *Erk*; he has stated that the party is "for strong presidential power and for the policies of the popularly elected president because if we go against him, we go against the people."[1]

Clans

When Uzbekistan was part of the Soviet Union, politics often boiled down to competition among essentially three regionally based clans, from the city of Tashkent, the Fergana Valley, and the Samarkand-Jizzakh areas. All the previous first secretaries of the republic's Communist Party were from one of these three regions. However, the 1980s cotton scandal and the emergence of Karimov dealt a blow to the clans' influence from which they have not fully recovered. The most visible break with the clans has been a gov-

---

1. *Segodnia*, February 24, 1994.

ernment-sponsored campaign against former Vice President Shukurullo Mirsaidov, a leading representative of the Tashkent clan and, more generally, the old elite, beginning in 1992.

Karimov has shown increased readiness to adopt the mantle of the Samarkand-Jizzakh clan. He has initiated a campaign to rehabilitate the image of the republic's longtime Communist Party first secretary, Sharif Rashidov, a native of Jizzakh, and has granted amnesty to prominent members of the Samarkand clan who were involved in the cotton scandal.

Karimov has consolidated personal authority largely at the expense of the clan system. Not surprisingly given their history of competition, the various regional clans have neither united to challenge his control over the republican government nor succeeded in reassuming positions of influence within government structures.

Islam

In contrast to the other major Turkic peoples of Central Asia, the Uzbeks settled several centuries ago and hence became more imbued with both the mainstream Sunni Islamic culture and the mystical Sufi movements of the region's cities and towns. Despite Uzbekistan's 70 years of official atheism, Islam, particularly in its conservative Sunni form, has remained an important social and cultural factor among Uzbeks and the Tajik minority, especially in the Fergana Valley and the city of Bukhara. In some instances Islam has taken on a political character in recent years, causing consternation in the government. Although it is generally supportive of Islam's revival because of its role in the Uzbeks' heritage, the Karimov government has cracked down on several Islamic movements on the grounds that they destabilize society.

Islam has two organizational forms in Uzbekistan: official Islam, headed by the government-sanctioned Spiritual Board of Muslims in Tashkent, and unofficial local Muslim groups that are autonomous. The Spiritual Board is a construct of the Soviet era that was charged with leading all of Central Asia's Muslims, a jurisdiction that has been reduced to Uzbekistan since the dissolution of the USSR. With widely reputed links to the government and the KGB, the board was a means of holding Muslim political ambitions or discontent in check. Its location in Tashkent, the republic's political capital, rather than in one of the great historic centers of Islamic culture in Central Asia such as Bukhara, reflects this purpose.

After a period of leadership by a relatively independent-minded head *mufti* from 1989 to 1993, the board is once again an agency that is thoroughly loyal to the government and serves as a brake on anti-government sentiments based on religion. The previous *mufti*, Muhammad Sadyk Muhammad Yusuf, resigned under government pressure and was replaced by an apolitical figure whose deputy, Bobokhan, was Muhammad Sadyk's predecessor as head of the Spiritual Board.

In addition to the board, there are independent Islamic movements in the Fergana Valley. As in Tajikistan, outsiders to the movements have dubbed them *"Wahabi."* These groups, most notably *Adolat* (Justice) and *Islom Lashkari* (Warriors of Islam), have focused on policing petty crime and what they consider lapses in public morality. They call for—and in some cases have physically enforced—greater observance of Islamic norms among the Muslims in their regions.

Local in focus, the groups have not opposed President Karimov directly, although they have criticized the government for not being Islamic enough. Furthermore, there is reportedly little coordination, and, in some cases, even friction, among the various groups, which lessens the challenge they pose to the Karimov government. Nonetheless, their tapping of the potentially powerful force of Islam, along with their independent authority and perceived disruption of civic order, prompted government crackdowns beginning in late 1991. *Adolat* earned further disfavor by organizing a noisy protest and forcing its demands on Karimov while he was in Namangan in November 1991. The groups lead a semi-underground existence, although most of their members are at large and loose structures remain.

Finally, in addition to the local groups, there existed a national religiously oriented organization, the Islamic Renaissance Party (IRP), based out of the Fergana Valley. The government has banned the IRP since 1992. Like its counterpart in Tajikistan, it made relatively moderate public statements, avoiding calls for the immediate introduction of the *shariat* (Islamic law) or a takeover of government. However, the combination of political Islam, national scope, and the activism of Tajikistan's IRP aroused deep suspicion in a government determined to maintain domination. The IRP's chairman, Abdullah Utaev, disappeared in December 1992 and is widely believed to be under detention.

Interethnic Relations

Like all of the Central Asian republics, Uzbekistan is home to several minorities. The country has witnessed numerous cases of ethnic violence in recent history: pogroms against small populations of Mesketian Turks and Armenians in the cities of Fergana and Andijan respectively, where their trading in local markets aroused discontent, and bloody fighting between Kyrgyz and Uzbeks in neighboring Osh Oblast in the Kyrgyz Republic. Preventing such conflicts has been one of President Karimov's main justifications for what he admits are often authoritarian measures against the opposition.

The republic's largest minority is the Russian population, which makes up about 8 percent of the population and is concentrated in industrial cities (over half the Russians reside in Tashkent).

ethnic breakdown
Uzbek, 71.4%
Russian, 8.3%
Tajik, 4.7%
Kazakh, 4.1%
Tatar, 2.4%
Karakalpak, 2.1 %
Other, 7.0%

As in other republics, Russians express concern over perceived ethnic discrimination and uncertainty over their own and their children's future. Disaffected Russians are trying to emigrate to Russia instead of pressing their complaints in Uzbekistan. At the same time, financial considerations play a major role in determining Russians' readiness to leave: the rate of Russian emigration was relatively small until Uzbekistan's economy took a steep downturn in the second half of 1993.

Pressure from Moscow over ethnic Russians' rights irked the Karimov government, which long denied that the country's Russian population had any real problems. The nadir in Russian-Uzbekistani differences was reached when Russian Foreign Minister Andrei Kozyrev arrived in Tashkent to lecture a very irritated President Karimov on Russians' rights in mid-November 1993.

Relations between the two states have improved since Kozyrev's November visit, and the government's stance toward its

Russian population has changed. At a meeting with Yeltsin in Moscow in early March 1994, Karimov signed an agreement on a joint Uzbek-Russian committee to work out ways of resolving concerns among the Russians living in Uzbekistan. At the same time, Karimov has avoided any concessions to Russian pressure on dual citizenship; in any case, Uzbekistani legislation expressly forbids it.

Uzbekistan faces a potentially much more volatile problem with its Tajik population centered in Bukhara and Samarkand. Many of the grounds for conflict are rooted in the murky history of interethnic divisions. In the fifteenth century, Turkic nomadic tribes, including Uzbeks, seized power over the area between the Amu Darya and Syr Darya and most of Central Asia's urban centers, including the great cities of Samarkand and Bukhara. These cities were inhabited by a mixture of ancient sedentary populations that had absorbed and been absorbed by successive waves of nomadic invaders over the centuries, but were united by a common Persian culture. Like previous nomadic conquerors, the Uzbeks settled in the cities and adopted their culture (Uzbeks who settled in rural areas retained more elements of their Turkic culture, including language). Modern Uzbeks claim to be the end product of the region's mixing of peoples. Farsi-speaking modern Tajiks, on the other hand, claim to be the descendants of the region's ancient city dwellers, distinct from the Turkic Uzbek newcomers.

The differences were accented when the Bolsheviks created the separate republics of Tajikistan and Uzbekistan in the 1920s. Samarkand and Bukhara, the centers of Central Asia's urban Persian culture, were incorporated into Uzbekistan. In order to solidify its holdings, the republic embarked on a campaign of Uzbekification by registering citizens as Uzbeks and mandating the use of Uzbek language in administration. This has resulted in an officially very small Tajik population of under 10 percent in Samarkand and Bukhara, although Tajik remains the cities' basic language. However, the distinction is both confusing and arbitrary; in both cities one encounters persons for whom Tajik is the preferred language but who consider themselves Uzbek and self-declared Tajiks who study in Uzbek-language schools and are Uzbek according to their internal passports.

Encouraged by glasnost in the late 1980s, some Tajiks began to express resentment over Uzbek inroads. A loose cultural association named "Samarkand" was set up in 1989 to press for Tajiks' rights. For almost two years, it waged an aggressive local campaign to allow citizens whose internal passports designated them as Uzbeks to re-register as Tajiks.

Tajik demands in Samarkand and Bukhara carried special significance because of the deep resonance of the issue in Tajikistan proper. The general awakening of national consciousness across the Soviet Union in the late 1980s prompted Tajiks in Tajikistan to look toward their historic centers in Samarkand and Bukhara. In 1990 and 1991, some Tajiks even proposed uniting the two "Tajik" cities with the republic.

Events have since worked against the Tajik movements. First, Tajikistan slid into a civil war that led to the formation of a government reliant on Tashkent for support and therefore in no position to raise the issue. Second, President Karimov consolidated authority in Uzbekistan and began to crack down on Tajik movements beginning in the summer of 1991. "Samarkand" ceased to exist by 1993, and its chairman, after several arrests, publicly renounced its doings in the winter of 1994. Nonetheless, the blurry Tajik-Uzbek distinction remains a source of potential friction, especially since it has ramifications outside of Uzbekistan.

The Fergana Valley

Challenges to President Karimov's control are most potent in the Fergana Valley, a mostly agricultural area slightly smaller than New Jersey in the republic's east. Separated from Uzbekistan's capital by a mountain range, the area has traditionally resisted domination from Tashkent. Partly for this reason, *Birlik* cells have flourished in the area. More important, the valley is the most strongly Muslim area in the republic and arguably in all of Central Asia.

Populated by a mixture of Uzbeks, Tajiks, Kyrgyz, and several other smaller populations, the valley is also a flash point for ethnic conflict for all of Central Asia. The ethnic jumble is further complicated by the fact that the valley's fringes are the territory of the Kyrgyz Republic or Tajikistan, precipitating interrepublican administrative disputes over land and especially water use. Several ethnic disturbances have already occurred in the valley over the past decade.

Finally, as home to a young and rapidly growing population of 5 million people, the region faces difficulties owing to an increasing scarcity of land, housing, and jobs. Economic discontent fuels ethnic tensions within the valley as well as political and religious radicalism directed against the central government. There is widespread foreboding in Tashkent that the situation in the Fergana Valley will explode. For this reason, President Karimov has been much more cautious in the Fergana Valley than in Tashkent about cracking down on opposition.

ECONOMICS

Material Assets Profile

While it does not have the huge oil fields of Kazakhstan or gas reserves of Turkmenistan, Uzbekistan is blessed with significant deposits of both, plus a wealth of other minerals. Uzbekistan currently imports about half of its oil and other petroleum products (ironically, almost entirely from Russia and not from its Central Asian neighbor Kazakhstan), but in 1992 it found a rich new field that should increase domestic oil extraction to a level nearing self-sufficiency by 1996. Oil production (4 million metric tons in 1993) is limited to the Fergana Valley. Uzbekistan also extracts large amounts of gas (45 million metric tons in 1993). Nonetheless, the country is constrained by the distribution system to import gas from Turkmenistan for its western population, while it exports larger amounts of gas to the Kyrgyz Republic and Russia. Uzbekistan mines small amounts of coal.

Uzbekistan possesses the second largest gold deposits in the former Soviet Union, after Russia. Deposits are concentrated in the large Muruntau field in the north-central section of the country. Several Western companies have already set up joint ventures to develop the country's gold fields. Uzbekistan is also home to large deposits of tungsten, copper, lead, zinc, and manganese. The country mines marble and other construction materials.

Benefiting from the waters of the Amu Darya and the Syr Darya, Uzbekistan is a major agricultural producer, although it faces severe difficulties as a result of environmental degradation. Cotton is Uzbekistan's most important crop, with over 4 million metric tons of raw cotton produced in 1993; however, the government is encouraging the reduction of cotton fields to lessen the strain on the environment and promote more balanced domestic production. In addition to cotton, the republic produces silk, rice, fruits, and vegetables in large quantities. Uzbekistan used to be a major wine producer; its vineyards are making a slow comeback after most of them were destroyed under Gorbachev's anti-alcohol campaign in the mid-1980s. The republic relies on imports of potatoes and wheat, mostly from Russia and Kazakhstan, respectively.

Uzbekistan has some textile plants, although most of its cotton is woven in Russia. The republic also has a limited amount of heavy industry, primarily for processing locally extracted metals. There are also several chemical plants that produce fertilizers and pharmaceuticals. The machinery industry, including the enormous Chkalov aircraft plant, is directly tied into the former Soviet Union's economy and hence has suffered greatly. Most heavy industry is centered in Tashkent. As in neighboring Kazakhstan and the Kyrgyz Republic, the problems related to heavy industry are compounded by ethnic issues, since the labor force is mostly Russian.

Performance in 1993

True to its policy of promoting stability above all else, Uzbekistan's government spent most of 1993 trying to preserve the social safety net and job security of the old Soviet system. President Karimov frequently pointed to the chaotic course of market reforms and consequent political tensions in Russia as proof positive that the old system should be changed very gradually. Subsidies to industry and agriculture remained at high levels, prices were largely controlled, and state management ensured that goods were put on the shelves. A visit to Tashkent in October 1993 left the impression that Uzbekistan was more similar to the Soviet Union of the early 1980s than any other republic except perhaps Turkmenistan. Karimov also worked hard—though unsuccessfully—to maintain the rouble zone with Russia, Kazakhstan, and other CIS states in an effort to preserve the Soviet-era links among the republics' economies.

Official statistics reflect the relative resilience of Uzbekistan's economy in 1993. The republic experienced a 3.5 percent drop in GDP, with a 7 percent drop in industrial production and a 0.3 percent drop in agricultural production. These figures are the second lowest in the entire CIS, after Turkmenistan. While economic indicators generated in the former Soviet Union and especially in Central Asia must be taken with a grain of salt, the figures are probably accurate at least relative to other republics, since Uzbekistan's industry is less dependent on the rest of the CIS than Kazakhstan's or the Kyrgyz Republic's and the country has not endured the civil strife of Tajikistan.

The policy of preserving state-managed economics came apart at the end of 1993 as the government found it increasingly difficult to subsidize prices and became more and more concerned about the viability of the rouble zone. The deathblow came when Uzbekistan was forced to leave the rouble zone in November. Although the country had contemplated introducing its own currency long before (banknotes were already printed in 1992), it was clearly caught off guard. The Uzbekistani government hastily introduced a transitional currency, the *sum* (pronounced "soom") coupon, to function alongside the old Soviet roubles beginning in November 15. By January, the temporary *sum* coupon had become essentially the only currency. Confidence in the currency is low: its black market exchange rate jumped from about 3,000 to the dollar in mid-November 1993 to 8,000 (roughly five times the 1993 rouble-to-dollar rate for the same period) in late January 1994. On July 1, 1994, Uzbekistan completed the transition by introducing the permanent *sum*, although there was criticism that the currency lacked the necessary backing to remain stable.

Although the state had already begun to increase prices relative to average wages, the *sum*'s introduction marked a significant hike in prices. According to official statistics, after a year of some of the CIS's lowest figures, the monthly price index on a basket of basic consumer goods jumped during each of the final three months of 1993 by 29.7 percent, 59.7 percent, and 56.5 percent, respectively.

Tashkent responded in December 1993 by changing course to pursue market reforms more vigorously. President Karimov has established a high-profile economic reform council and appointed reform-oriented economists to head up the country's National Bank and Ministry of Finance. He has issued several decrees in December 1993 and January 1994 to spur market development and foreign investment. Measures reportedly include the legalization of buying and selling land (including to foreigners), reduction of import tariffs until July 1, 1995, and exemption of joint ventures with a foreign majority share from taxation on their hard currency earnings if they produce consumer goods.

The Uzbekistani government remains reluctant to begin large-scale privatization, aside from the already largely implemented privatization of individual dwellings. The government greatly fears the social consequences of labor layoffs from privatized collective farms and industrial plants.

Non-CIS Involvement

Uzbekistan's large, undersupplied consumer market has drawn significant foreign interest, although the volume of foreign investment is still not very high. By the end of 1993, there were more than 900 joint ventures in Uzbekistan, mostly based in manufacturing and retail trade. As elsewhere in Central Asia, the largest number of joint ventures are with Chinese and Turkish partners. Turkish firms have been particularly active in developing ventures in the republic's cotton industry. Cheap Uzbekistani cotton allows textile plants in Turkey to compete better on the world market.

In contrast to Kazakhstan, Uzbekistan has signed only a few, fairly small deals with foreign partners to develop its extractive industries. However, with the government's recent measures to encourage greater foreign investment, it is expected that the republic will more actively seek foreign partners for these sectors.

FOREIGN RELATIONS

Like all other post-Soviet republics, Uzbekistan's paramount relationship is with Russia. Tashkent has found common ground with Moscow on keeping the region free of foreign political influences that might disrupt the status quo. For its part, Russia seems content to work with and through Uzbekistan, the strongest power in Central Asia, to preempt major changes in the region's geopolitics. This marriage of interests is seen most clearly in the countries' cooperation on Tajikistan.

The close relationship was tested in the fall of 1993, when Russia applied heavy pressure on the Karimov government over ethnic Russians' rights and forced Uzbekistan out of the rouble zone. However, talks between Karimov and Yeltsin in Moscow in March 1994 smoothed relations. Karimov has committed himself to addressing problems faced by Uzbekistan's ethnic Russians, but even more important to Moscow, he has advocated a strong Russian presence in Central Asia, calling it the "guarantor of stability" in the region. Russia reportedly has responded by agreeing to continue exporting oil to Uzbekistan at levels similar to those in 1993.

Uzbekistan is the key local power in Central Asia. The country's geographic centrality is extremely important given the haphazardness of the borders drawn by the Bolsheviks: though the Central Asian republics have confirmed the inviolability of almost all current borders, there is a potential dispute between Uzbekistan and each of its neighbors except Afghanistan. Furthermore, significant portions of the Kyrgyz Republic, Turkmenistan, and Tajikistan are tied into Uzbekistan's economy.

Uzbekistan's leadership also derives from the fact that it is the most populous republic (with over 21 million people) in the region. Kazakhstan is the only other Central Asian state comparable in terms of population; however, it is geographically and ethnically split between association with Central Asia and Russia's Siberia and Ural regions. In addition, the Uzbeks are by far the largest ethnic group in Central Asia, with over 15 million people in the republic and over 2.5 million combined in Tajikistan, the Kyrgyz Republic, Turkmenistan, and Kazakhstan (making up 25 percent, 12.9 percent, 9 percent, and 2.1 percent of the other republics' populations, respectively). There are another 2.5 million

Uzbeks in Afghanistan. By comparison, the 9 million Russians are the second largest ethnic group in Central Asia; Kazakhs run third, with about 8 million total.

Uzbekistan enjoys good relations with Kazakhstan and Turkmenistan, perhaps in part owing to their leaders' shared backgrounds in the Communist-era bureaucracy. As by far the two largest countries in the region, Uzbekistan and Kazakhstan have shown some rivalry. However, their governments demonstrated a high level of cooperation in dealing with Russia over the rouble zone and again when introducing their own currencies. They also initiated the tariff-free, customs-free common market in February 1994. Uzbekistan and Turkmenistan have avoided clashes over the usage of water from the Amu Darya river, though this will be a growing problem.

Relations with the Kyrgyz Republic have been problematic in the past on account of differences between Karimov and Kyrgyz President Akaev on political openness and the pace of economic reform. The most bitter moment was when Karimov closed all borders and cut off electricity and gas to the southern part of the Kyrgyz Republic in retaliation for its break with the rouble zone in May 1993. Karimov turned the switches and pipes back on only when Akaev went to Tashkent, apologized, and promised to compensate for the flood of roubles being spent in Uzbekistan. Relations have since improved. Significantly, Karimov went to Bishkek in January 1994 to sign agreements allowing the Kyrgyz Republic to enter into the Uzbekistan-Kazakhstan common market.

Uzbekistan is heavily involved in war-stricken Tajikistan, having reportedly provided arms, training, artillery, air power, and even troops to the winning side. It continues to provide extensive technical and material support to the government in Dushanbe as well as to the autonomous regional authorities in northern Leninabad Oblast. Uzbekistani authorities claim that its actions are only the natural reaction to a situation "where a neighbor's house is burning down." However, in addition to quelling Tajikistan's domestic conflict, Tashkent also clearly aims to ensure that the Tajik nationalist and Islamic sentiments that united sections of the losing side do not prevail, lest they spread to Uzbekistan.

The Karimov government maintains a close relationship with ethnic Uzbek General Abdul Rashid Dostam's faction in northern Afghanistan. Uzbekistan provides at least material support to Dostam's faction and reportedly even shelters his children in Tashkent. Afghanistan's official government has accused Uzbekistan of also supplying weapons to Dostam, including much of the firepower he unleashed on Kabul during the latest round of fighting in the winter of 1994. President Karimov has vigorously denied this charge.

Despite Uzbekistan's undoubted local influence, the republic cannot play an independent role as regional heavyweight for now because Russia remains the preeminent economic and strategic power throughout post-Soviet Central Asia. Tashkent must always act within the broad outlines of Russia's strategic goals. For instance, Russia let Uzbekistan do a lot of the dirty work during Tajikistan's civil war; however, when Moscow began to call for negotiations between the Tajik government and the opposition, Tashkent was forced to follow suit, though it was unhappy about compromising with the Tajik opposition.

Uzbekistan has relatively poor intergovernmental relations with the West and particularly the United States, owing to Washington's criticism of the republic's human rights record. However, though defensive about its domestic policy, Uzbekistan's leadership is eager to take advantage of new opportunities to set up direct contacts. Recognizing that its crackdowns have won few political friends, Tashkent has focused on encouraging Western businesses to invest in the republic and developing cultural contacts.

Foreign Influence in Central Asia

After decades of isolation, Central Asia has suddenly become open to contacts with the rest of the world. Countries in the vicinity are jockeying to spread their influence in the newly accessible region. However, the contemporary struggle for influence in Central Asia bears little resemblance to the nineteenth-century "Great Game" between Russia and Britain for control over South Asia. Given Russia's continued domination, the new players in the region— Turkey, Iran, Pakistan, and China—are at most putting up their antes for a game that is just beginning. Furthermore, whereas in the past the technologically more advanced European powers were able to impose their influence with limited investment of money and manpower, some of the current players are less developed than the Central Asian countries. Although Russia's presence may recede, none of its competitors, except perhaps for China, appears likely to have the capacity to project its will on Central Asia.

The growing links between Central Asia's republics and the outside world are nonetheless important as an antidote to the extreme orientation toward Russia that has caused so many problems. While preserving close ties to Russia remains their main priority, Central Asia's leaders are eager to develop or renew cultural, economic, and political contacts with other countries in the region and the industrialized West.

TURKEY

Much like the myth of Central Asian unity, there has been a widespread assumption that Kazakhstan, the Kyrgyz Republic, Turkmenistan, and Uzbekistan, whose indigenous peoples mostly speak a language related to Turkish, were destined to have a special association with Turkey on the basis of geographic proximity and shared cultural and historical roots. Furthermore, many in the West and Turkey believed that the newly independent Central Asian states would be attracted to Ankara's secular model and record of economic progress during the 1980s. Eager to discern a bloc of allies, Turkish politicians vigorously promoted this vision in the heady days following the republics' declarations of independence. Regional maps with Turkey, Azerbaijan (a mainly Turkic republic in the Caucasus), Kazakhstan, the Kyrgyz Republic, Turkmenistan, and Uzbekistan all shaded with the same color began rolling off Turkish presses.

Central Asia's closeness to Turkey was clearly exaggerated even before the first official from Ankara arrived in the region. First, Central Asia is separated from Turkey by two major barriers: the Caspian Sea and the mountainous, strife-ridden Caucasus region. Second, Anatolia and Central Asia were part of a united state only very briefly under Timur in the beginning of the fifteenth century; Central Asia was never part of the Ottoman Empire and therefore does not arouse popular sentiment in Turkey as do territories formerly ruled by Istanbul such as Bosnia or Azerbaijan. Third, the Turkic peoples inhabiting Central Asia split off from the Turks of Anatolia more than a millennium ago (although there are now some Turks with distinctly Uzbek or Kazakh roots living in modern Turkey). An inhabitant of Ankara finds it hard to hold a conversation with anyone in Central Asia with the partial exception of the Turkmens; as one travels farther from Turkey, the differences between the local language and Turkish grow. Finally, as one Turkish diplomat privately noted, the Central Asians are so Russified (at least in the cities) that there is little cultural closeness between the populations.

Whatever the gap between myth and reality, the Turks are motivated and equipped as well as any outside power to stake out a political and economic role in the region. When Central Asia became independent, Turkey had much clearer ideas than other states seeking influence in the area about what it wanted to achieve: to increase cultural unity in the Turkic world; to benefit from the region's resources; and to serve as an intermediary between the region and the rest of the world, both as a transit route for pipelines carrying Central Asia's oil and gas and as the leader of the Turkic world. Turkey was quickest off the mark in setting up large embassies and sending high-level delegations to the region.

Ankara has launched several measures to build cultural ties with the region. Several hours of Turkish television beam into the Turkic Central Asian republics every day. Turkey offered 2,000 scholarships apiece to Kazakhstan, the Kyrgyz Republic, Turkmenistan, and Uzbekistan in 1993, although not all of these were accepted. Private Turkish schools, in some cases run by Turks, are springing up everywhere.

The keystone of Ankara's cultural expansion has been the promotion of the Latin alphabet to replace the Cyrillic currently used to render the Turkic languages of the region. The four mostly Turkic republics signed an agreement with Ankara to make the switch, although only Turkmenistan has begun to implement it by eschewing Cyrillic on its new currency, the *manat*. As when the Bolsheviks forced the Central Asian peoples to switch from the Arabic script to Latin characters and then to the Cyrillic alphabet in the 1920s and 1930s, the symbolic and long-term effect of this shift would be a sharp break with the past. The measure would wrench the area out of Russia's cultural orbit and open the floodgates to the influx of Turkish literature and culture into the region. Perhaps even more significantly, it would also make Western computer technology and networks more relevant and available.

The change of alphabet will not be easy. The high literacy rates and level of education that the Central Asian republics achieved over the past half century will suddenly be greatly undercut. The move is certain to alienate the Russian community, causing problems with Moscow and in local industry. (This is a major reason why Kazakhstan, with over 40 percent of its population consisting of Russian-speakers, delayed even considering the agreement's ratification in parliament.) Finally, and perhaps most important, the cost of transliterating libraries, textbooks, government documents, and street signs will be enormous. Relatively prosperous Turkmenistan feels confident enough of its finances to pursue such reform; less well-off Kazakhstan, the Kyrgyz Republic, and Uzbekistan have refrained from any serious measures as of yet, mainly because of the costs involved.

Turkish firms rushed into Central Asia in 1991 to stake out new markets and especially new sources of raw materials in the resource-rich region. At the end of 1993, Turkish entities were the second most frequent non-CIS partners in joint ventures in Kazakhstan, the Kyrgyz Republic, and Uzbekistan (the first being China) and the most common such partner in Turkmenistan. Turkish firms have been particularly active in developing wool and leather processing in Kazakhstan and the Kyrgyz Republic, and textile production from Uzbekistani and Turkmenistani cotton.

The Turkish government is by far the single largest outside aid donor to the region (if one does not consider the special case of Russian credits) and likes to think of itself as a model for Central Asia. Turkey spearheaded the acceptance of the Central Asian republics into the Economic Cooperation Organization (ECO) in 1992. Central Asia's leaders have responded in kind to the rhetoric surrounding Turkey's initiatives—especially when they involve investment. However, these leaders express similar eagerness to renew links with long-lost friends in other countries in the region, such as Pakistan or Iran, and are also hungry for exposure to the industrialized world. Finally, as persons schooled in the Soviet system, Central Asia's leaders are keenly aware that their key relationship for the foreseeable future is with Russia.

More than two years of relations have highlighted Turkey's limitations: Turkey obviously lacks the capital and technology that Central Asia needs most. Although deals have been cut with Turkish partners, few involve significant amounts of capital. Total trade between Central Asia and Turkey amounts to only a few hundred million dollars. Furthermore, Central Asia's republics do not look to Turkish technology when seeking partners in developing their crucial extractive industries.

Turkey's limitations also preclude it from becoming an intermediary between the region and the West. Similarly, it is unlikely that Turkey can overcome adverse geography and become a conduit for Central Asia's oil and gas (though its control of the Black Sea outlet gives it more leverage with Russia on this score). Cultural ties will naturally continue to grow, but it remains to be seen if the republics carry out the momentous change to Latin script. Many Central Asian officials are irritated by Ankara's self-designated role as a leader and model for the region. Central Asians do not seem anxious to trade a Russian big brother for a Turkish one, even if they could. Moreover, having been integral parts of one of the world's two superpowers, these countries are unwilling to follow the leadership of Turkey, a country still cooling its heels outside the European Union. Furthermore, Turkey's parliamentary democracy holds little interest for the authoritarian leaders of most of Central Asia's republics. When looking for a model, these leaders find more politically and economically attractive versions among the Asian tigers or China.

Turkey has grown conscious of its weaknesses and scaled back its expectations of relations with the republics in the area. Furthermore, Turkish politicians and business leaders have found their Turkic brethren in Central Asia far more different—and far more tied to Russia—than they had anticipated.

Ankara has also reassessed the geopolitics of its commitment to laying a claim for influence in the area. Just as Turkey is not the only nearby country of interest to Central Asia, the Turkic republics are not the only objects of Turkish attention in the former Soviet Union. In fact, Russia itself has proved to be Turkey's major economic partner in the region. When the USSR began to open up, Turkish firms were among the first to go to Moscow; Russia's government engaged these firms to do most of the restoration of Russia's parliament building after it was damaged in October 1993. Turkey imports natural gas from Russia and not, ironically, from its closest neighbor in Central Asia, Turkmenistan (a function of how the pipelines work in the former Soviet Union; Ashgabat cannot increase its current quotas of gas going through these pipelines).

Both Turkey and the Central Asian republics must exercise care in building ties lest they upset their crucial relationships with Moscow. When the Central Asian states attended an ECO meeting in Istanbul in July 1993 at which a regional common market was discussed, Moscow responded flatly that the former Soviet republics would have to choose between it and ECO (knowing full well that none of the republics could afford to cut off ties with Russia).

For its part, Ankara has made it clear that it is not prepared to go out on a limb for Central Asia. Turkey's Prime Minister Tansu Ciller reportedly even stated during a visit in Moscow in November 1993 that Ankara had "given up its claims" on Central Asia.[1]

Despite the undoubted energy that accompanied its push into the area, Turkey is economically and politically unable to play a dominant role as regional power in Central Asia. Although Turkey maintains overall the strongest presence of all the non-Russian players in Central Asia, its ties with the region are unlikely to translate into much special influence, let alone dominance.

IRAN

Iran has several important historical and cultural bonds with Central Asia. The most obvious link is with the 4.5 million ethnic Tajiks who live in the area; unlike the Turkic peoples of Central Asia, who speak languages that are often quite distinct from modern Turkish, Tajiks speak a dialect of Farsi (Persian) that is intelligible to Iranians. The culture and language of the great cities of Central Asia, such as Bukhara, Samarkand, and Khiva, were Persian until the advent of Soviet rule in the twentieth century. To this day the language spoken on the streets in Samarkand and Bukhara, whatever the ethnic composition of their inhabitants, is Tajik/Farsi. These cities as well as Merv, now in ruins in Turkmenistan, occupy an important place in Iranian historical memory.

There is, however, one crucial distinction between the peoples of Central Asia and Iran: the former are mostly Sunni and bear the effects of 70 years of atheistic rule, while the latter are Shiite. In fact, Tajiks are distinguished from Iranians mainly by their religious differences. The current theocratic regime in Tehran further underscores the divisions caused by religion, as Central Asia's secular governments and many among its urban elites are opposed to Islam's domination of society and especially its politicization.

Iran has a special link with Turkmenistan, the only Central Asian country with which it shares a border. Much of modern Turkmenistan was ruled by Persian shahs until Russia moved into the region. In addition, the 615-mile border separates well over 1

---

1. Cited by *Inter Press Service*, November 8, 1993.

million Turkmens in Iran from the approximately 2.5 million Turkmens in Turkmenistan proper (there are also a few thousand Iranians in the Central Asian republic). Many of these Turkmens are now resurrecting family ties that were cut for 70 years when the Soviet Union sealed off the border.

The geographic link with Iran is more important than the historic one, as Central Asia seeks new trade routes with the outside world. Even if trading through Russia were entirely secure and smooth, Iran provides a shorter route to the open seas for Central Asia's exports, including Turkmenistani gas. The development of this option may be hindered by Iran's current international standing, but in the long run Central Asia has few choices.

Iran's policy toward Central Asia is determined by how it balances the three elements of its relationship to the region: its radical Islamic ideology, cultural ties, and economic and geopolitical interests. At present, Tehran clearly favors the last. Central Asia presents too many potential benefits to warrant upsetting its governments by an aggressive campaign to support Islamic revolution. In any case, Sunni Central Asia is far more susceptible to religious influence from Saudi Arabia and Pakistan. Iranian officials frequently seek to reassure Central Asia about Iran's aims in the region; its ambassador in Tashkent stated that his country has "no intention of spreading Islam in Uzbekistan."[2]

Iran's stance toward Tajikistan demonstrates these policy priorities. Although it has had ties to the Islamist opposition and Tajikistan's religious leader-in-exile spends a good deal of time in Tehran, Iran has generally kept a low profile over the republic's civil conflict, especially after Russia asserted itself there. Tehran has sought to strengthen its cultural presence, most notably by persuading Tajikistan to switch from the current Cyrillic rendering of its language to the Persian script, although the republic does not currently have the financial means to follow through. According to Tajikistani officials, the most active contacts between the two countries are in education, not trade or diplomacy.

Iranian officials have been careful not to overstate cultural affinity with other, mainly Turkic Central Asian nations. In particular, while noting the Persian contribution to the development

---

2. *Agence France Presse*, October 18, 1993.

of cities in the region, Iran has avoided involvement in the Tajik-Uzbek debate over claims to Bukhara and Samarkand.

The October 1993 visit of President Rafsanjani confirmed Iran's relatively pragmatic approach toward Central Asia. Rafsanjani traveled to the four Turkic republics, skipping controversial Tajikistan. His entourage included Iran's foreign minister, economics minister, transport minister, and members of the business community. The visit resulted in the conclusion of several economic development deals. Agreements were reached concerning oil and gas extraction; with its own experience in this sector, Iran is better suited than its rivals Turkey and Pakistan to develop these key industries. Second, and more important, Iran pledged to accelerate work on its section of a proposed rail link connecting the northern Iranian city of Mashhad with Central Asia's railroads at the Turkmenistani city of Tajan, as well as to upgrade facilities on the Caspian Sea to receive shipping from Kazakhstan and Turkmenistan. The inauguration of weekly flights between Tehran and Tashkent during the visit highlighted Iran's emphasis on improving physical links with the region.

For their part, Central Asia's governments appreciated Iran's diplomacy, not only because Tehran made clear that it is not trying to export its political and social model to the region, but also because the economic agreements signed during the visit responded directly to some of Central Asia's pressing needs. In the eyes of many in the Central Asian republics, Iran's low-key approach compares favorably to Turkey's heavy-handed arrogation of a special, leading role as a model for the area. Rafsanjani's first visit, coming two years after the region's republics became independent, successfully cemented the relationship. When he arrived in Turkmenistan, thousands reportedly lined the streets to meet him and a mosque was dedicated in his name.

The economic logic of the region's geography, not religious fervor or cultural expansion, is the motor of the relationship between Iran and Central Asia. If Tehran maintains its current ideological restraint and relations with Russia continue to present problems for Central Asia, the republics in the region will place increasing importance on ties to Iran and the access to the open seas which they provide.

PAKISTAN

Separated from Central Asia by the massive mountains of the Hindu Kush in Afghanistan, the region that is now Pakistan has had fewer historical connections with the area than rivals Turkey or Iran. Although Babur, founder of the Moghul Dynasty that ruled northern India for three centuries, was originally from Andijan in Uzbekistan, the Indus Valley and Central Asia were never united for any length of time under the rule of a single state (Babur, a grandson of Timur, in fact moved south after losing power to the Uzbeks, who had emerged as rulers of Samarkand). The two areas were pushed farther apart during the nineteenth century, when Central Asia fell increasingly under Russian domination while the Indus Valley was controlled by the British. In this century, the isolation of the Soviet Union, its pro-India policy after the partition of India, and the antagonisms of the war in Afghanistan precluded meaningful contact until the Central Asian republics became independent in 1991.

Over the centuries, trade along the Silk Road bound the two regions together. Both have been eager to resurrect and update the old economic ties, spurred by modern incentives. Karachi is the best equipped of the warm-water seaports in the region, and much closer than any in Russia. Pakistan has much better relations than Iran with the industrialized West. Islamabad, motivated by the vision of a strategic, resource-rich Muslim "rear area" to strengthen its confrontation with India, moved rapidly to send delegations throughout Central Asia as soon as the doors were open.

As has been the case with Turkey and Iran, political and economic realities have tempered early euphoria and limited the influence that Pakistan can exert in Central Asia. Pakistan's conservative Sunni religious factions like *Jamaat-e-Islami* enjoy an advantage over secular Turkey and Shiite Iran in building mosques and training clerics in the region. But the allergy of Central Asian governments to imports of Islam's sectarianism has required Pakistan to soft-pedal its religious ties and focus on more practical relations. Politically, the Central Asian states do not share Pakistan's interest in a Muslim alliance aimed at India, even if this were feasible. On the contrary, as a result of the warm Indo-Soviet relations of past decades, all have close relations with India and want to maintain them. Kazakhstan's President Nazarbaev, for one, has good enough relations with both to offer himself as a mediator between India and Pakistan in their bitter dispute over Kashmir.

Afghanistan, the historic link between the steppes of Central Asia and the riches of the Indus Valley, remains the crux of Pakistan's access to the region. All the key land routes connecting the Khyber and Boland passes run through that mountainous, politically riven land. The achievement of stability is essential to the dream of large-scale Central Asian trade with the West via Karachi. The governments of the region—particularly Tajikistan, Turkmenistan, and Uzbekistan, which share borders with Afghanistan—value Pakistan's influence with the Afghan *mujahedeen* factions and its efforts to negotiate a settlement between them. Afghanistan has more ethnic Tajiks than Tajikistan itself. Dushanbe and Moscow, for that matter, appreciate Pakistan's appeals for a negotiated settlement to the Tajik civil war, as well as their offers to help mediate. But Pakistan has been no more successful than any other country in curbing the intense violence of factional rivalries inside Afghanistan, or bringing reconciliation to the Tajiks. There are persistent reports of support by Pakistani groups for different factions inside Afghanistan, including the Tajik opposition, even though the government has firmly disavowed such activity.

So far, the lack of stable land routes through Afghanistan has limited Pakistan's economic links to Central Asia to a few weekly flights connecting Islamabad, Tashkent, and Almaty. More numerous charter aircraft carry small-scale traders from Central Asia bearing dollars to Karachi and returning laden with consumer durables. Private direct investment deals have been talked about, but few have materialized as yet. Similarly, grand schemes to create transportation routes and finance public power projects are under discussion but lack the capital needed to make them real. Pakistan, for example, is committed to funding the completion of a hydroelectric plant in Tajikistan's Badakhshon region that will serve Pakistan's northern regions across Afghanistan's Wakhan corridor. When and if it materializes, this will be Islamabad's largest project in Central Asia. Turkmenistan and Pakistan have signed a communiqué to examine the feasibility of a natural gas pipeline and/or road from southern Turkmenistan through the relatively peaceful and flat terrain of western Afghanistan, but it must compete for attention with other gas routes under consideration. In an effort to avoid Afghanistan altogether, Pakistan has pressed neighboring China to improve the Xinjiang–Kyrgyz Republic portion of the road that connects Islamabad to Central Asia via Kashgar and the Karakorum highway. This route—remote from the main resources of the region—goes through high mountains and would only connect Pakistan to Kazakhstan between May and October each year.

CHINA

China's historic cultural ties with Central Asia are more limited than those of the other neighboring powers. In contrast to the other regional relationships, the direction of cultural contact has been more from Central Asia to China, via the Turkic Uygur, Kazakh, and Kyrgyz populations in China's Xinjiang Uygur Autonomous Region. But China's role in Central Asia, particularly in the neighboring countries of Kazakhstan and the Kyrgyz Republic, is hardly passive. With the major exception of Russia, China has a longer border with the combined area of the five republics and is a far greater power than any of its rivals. More important, China's historic role as economic partner and endpoint of the Silk Road has continuing significance today as Central Asia seeks to interact with the dynamic economy to its east.

Three elements have clouded China's political relations with Central Asia. First, decades of Sino-Soviet antagonism created deeply embedded fears that China, with its enormous population, would overrun the area. Disagreements remain over two sections of China's border with Kazakhstan and a portion of its border with Tajikistan—also holdovers from this standoff. However, all sides have agreed not to let border issues impede cooperation on a variety of other fronts, especially trade.

The second source of friction is continued Chinese testing of nuclear weapons at Lop Nor in Xinjiang, most recently in October 1993. These blasts affect the Kyrgyz Republic and Kazakhstan the most. Still suffering from the effects of Soviet nuclear testing in its Semipalatinsk region, at a site which it finally closed down a few years ago, Kazakhstan is particularly unhappy about China's actions. Kazakhstani officials in Almaty, less than 200 miles from the Chinese border, assert that these explosions are partly responsible for the high radiation levels in the eastern part of the country.

The third element is Beijing's fear that pan-Turkist or Islamic forces from Central Asia, or simply the example of the republics' independence, will fan separatist sentiments in its Xinjiang Uygur Autonomous Region. According to China's 1990 census, there are 7.2 million Uygurs along with 1.1 million Kazakhs and about 100,000 Kyrgyz in Xinjiang. These and other much smaller generally Turkic Muslim populations constitute as much as half the population of the region. Some underground movements among these peoples, especially the Uygurs, urge secession of the region, which they call East Turkestan, from Han-dominated China; over the past few years these groups have conducted a few bombings in Kashgar and elsewhere to press their cause. Separatist movements found a convenient base in the neighboring Central Asian states, particularly in Kazakhstan, where nearly 200,000 Uygurs reside (there also are about 30,000 Uygurs in both the Kyrgyz Republic and Uzbekistan). Until recently, Almaty allowed movements such as "Free East Turkestan" to operate on its territory.

The presence of significant numbers of Kazakhs and Kyrgyz on Chinese territory also has been a concern to Almaty and Bishkek, though neither is in a position to pressure its much larger eastern neighbor. Beijing's disinclination to allow the populations long split by the Sino-Soviet border to renew cultural contacts is an irritant to the relationships. Particularly galling was China's refusal to allow a delegation to attend a gathering of Kazakhs from all over the world in Almaty in March 1993, even though Xinjiang is home to the largest Kazakh population anywhere outside of Kazakhstan.

At the same time, economic relations took off as soon as Central Asia's republics became independent. China quickly emerged as the second most important trading partner (after Russia) for all of the Central Asian republics except for Turkmenistan. Cheap Chinese consumer goods flooded into Central Asia's starved markets, while bordering Kazakhstan and the Kyrgyz Republic exported large amounts of raw materials and industrial goods, especially steel, other metals, and fertilizers, to China. Many of these exports were in fact re-exports of items received from other members of the CIS (mostly Russia) at controlled prices or from barter arrangements set up to preserve the old planned-distribution system, then shipped across the border at a profit. On the Chinese side, the bulk of trade was limited to Xinjiang province. In the boom year of 1992, various statistics show at least $300-million and as much as $500-million worth of trade with Kazakhstan alone. Chinese firms have become by far the most common partners in joint ventures in Central Asia, although these agreements have brought in little investment. Finally, Chinese have reportedly been active in buying up property via straw men, especially in Kazakhstan and the Kyrgyz Republic.

Beginning in 1993, the dynamics of China's relationship with the Central Asian states began to change. Trade volume has fallen, though it remains significant. On the one hand, market factors are increasingly determining the nature of interrepublican trade in the former Soviet Union, making it harder for traders in Kazakhstan and the Kyrgyz Republic to obtain raw materials at low prices from Russia and elsewhere for re-export. Modest improvements in controls over border trade in these countries are also reducing the diversion of state-purchased goods for resale to China. On the other hand, demand for Chinese products has fallen. After rushing to buy cheap Chinese clothing and crockery, Central Asians now associate China with "shoddy goods." In addition to consumer dissatisfaction, there is a good deal of popular anxiety over Chinese purchases of real estate; this sentiment stems partly from the uncertainties surrounding property issues after decades of state ownership and partly, in all likelihood, from the insecurity of the Central Asian states about the intentions of their giant neighbor to the east.

The downturn in trade has contrasted with the development of warmer political relations between Beijing and the region. Central Asia's governments, especially in Almaty and Bishkek, recognize China's potential importance to the region as the only power that might compete with Russia (though Beijing has shown little inclination to do so as of yet). Furthermore, while unhappy with the current form of economic exchange, Central Asia's republics are eager to be a part of China's growing economy. Finally, China is yet another possible alternative to Russia as a route for Central

Asia's exports to the rest of the world. For its part, despite its anxiety about separatist sentiments in Xinjiang, Beijing is reassured by the fact that the governments that assumed power in newly independent Central Asia are hardly pan-Turkist or Islamic in outlook.

Beijing finally confirmed its official presence in the region during a ten-day visit by Premier Li Peng through Turkmenistan, Uzbekistan, the Kyrgyz Republic, and Kazakhstan in April 1994 (the visit had been planned a year earlier but was delayed, reportedly on account of Li's ill health). With the exception of testing at Lop Nor, progress was made on every key issue in the relationships between the Central Asian republics and China. Li spoke enthusiastically of recreating the Silk Road while promising that China would never seek hegemony in the region. In addition to offering modest new state credits, he reaffirmed China's pledge to improve its internal links with Xinjiang in order to serve as a conduit for Central Asian trade, including the addition of a second track along the railroad in Xinjiang connecting Kazakhstan to China's seaports. Li also signed a memorandum with Turkmenistan to study a project to build a pipeline from the desert republic across Central Asia and China to the Pacific. Finally, the Chinese leader stated that "the selling of shoddy or even fake products by some Chinese businessmen, mostly private, runs against the Chinese government's policy in this regard" and said that China is prepared to "draw up relevant measures so as to reduce the negative effect."[3]

Central Asia's republics were effusive in their eagerness to secure good relations with Beijing. Uzbekistan's President Karimov hailed China as "a great nation, a great people, and a great civilization."[4] More important, each of the Central Asian states pledged support for Beijing's efforts to quell separatist movements in Xinjiang Region, although whether they will crack down on cells in their own territory, especially Kazakhstan, remains unclear. Almaty banned Uygur groups from holding demonstrations during Li's visit.

---

3. *Xinhua News Agency*, April 27, 1994.
4. *Reuters*, April 28, 1994.

Of all the competitors for influence in Central Asia, China seems likely to become the strongest challenger to Russia's dominance of the region, especially in the Kyrgyz Republic and Kazakhstan (which are in many senses the most distant from Turkey or Iran). Although it lacks the technology or capital the republics need most, China's proximity, sheer size, and current rates of economic growth naturally attract the Central Asian republics. With deepening economic ties, political influence will follow. However, political influence will only come with time; as Li made very clear, China is not seeking to challenge Russia's political presence in Central Asia for now.

THE UNITED STATES

The United States has fewer ties with Central Asia than with the other subregions of the former Soviet Union; unlike Armenia or the Baltic republics, the new countries in the region do not have a significant American diaspora. Nonetheless, Central Asia is important to the United States because of its large mineral resources, the nuclear weapons in Kazakhstan, and its strategic location in the heart of the Eurasian landmass.

U.S. interests in Central Asia are threefold. First, the United States supports the development of democracy and free enterprise as keys to stability and growth in the republics, though it recognizes how hard it will be to develop these after decades of command economics and Communist Party rule, and, in the case of Tajikistan, the civil war. A related aim, particularly in the early stages when little was known about the region, has been to discourage the development of anti-Western Islamic fundamentalism in the area; the United States suggested to the Central Asian states that they follow the model of secular Turkey and steer clear of radical Iran. As it has throughout the former Soviet Union, the U.S. government has sponsored initiatives aimed at promoting democratic institutions and a market economy. The U.S. government has also been among the most vigorous in protesting violations of human rights in the republics of Central Asia, even to the point of souring relations with some of the region's governments.

Second, there is considerable American business interest in the region, particularly its mineral wealth. Kazakhstan has attracted by far the most investment, in terms of both numbers of firms and volume (more than 60 U.S. firms have offices in Almaty). The biggest deal involving foreign investment anywhere in the former Soviet Union is the $20 billion agreement that Chevron Oil signed with Kazakhstan in 1993. U.S. companies have also signed agreements worth hundreds of millions of dollars to exploit gold fields in Uzbekistan.

Third, and most pressing, the United States wants to ensure the security of weapons of mass destruction left in Central Asia after the USSR dissolved, particularly the 104 SS-18 nuclear ICBMs in Kazakhstan. These weapons are scheduled to be transported to Russia and destroyed under the START-II treaty that was signed in January 1993, but still awaits ratification. Although Kazakhstan seeks greater security guarantees and problems remain over compensation from Russia for the missiles' nuclear fuel, President Nazarbaev's government has eschewed any ambitions to become a nuclear state. Washington has welcomed Kazakhstan's pledge to join the Nuclear Nonproliferation Treaty as a non-nuclear state.

The pursuit of these objectives has led to the establishment of warm U.S. relations with the Kyrgyz Republic and Kazakhstan, the Central Asian countries perceived to have made the most progress in reforming their societies and observing human rights. In approval of Bishkek's reforming efforts, Washington has made the Kyrgyz Republic the highest per capita recipient of U.S. aid in the former Soviet Union (a modest amount, given that the republic's population is only 4.5 million). Aid to Kazakhstan is scheduled to jump from $91 million in 1993 to $311 million in 1994. Presidents Akaev and Nazarbaev were both received by President Bush, and the latter by President Clinton, in Washington, and they both hosted Vice President Gore in their respective capitals during his trip to Central Asia and Russia in December 1993.

Washington has markedly cooler relations with the governments of Tajikistan, Turkmenistan, and Uzbekistan because of these countries' civil liberties records. There has been a notable absence of high-level attention from the United States despite, in the case of the latter two, their size and wealth. Moreover, differences over human rights have marred visits by U.S. government officials and members of Congress to Uzbekistan and Turkmenistan.

Central Asia's republics attach great importance to their relationships with the United States. First, unlike the regional players, the United States has the capability to provide the capital and technology that Central Asia needs. Second, America's political weight as the world's remaining superpower is important to the Central Asian states as they try to find their own place in the global order. These countries are hungry for exposure and recognition in the West and especially the United States. Furthermore, Central Asia's leaders, particularly President Nazarbaev of Kazakhstan, appear to see ties with the United States as providing potential leverage against intervention by Russia.

The three-way relationship between the United States, the Central Asian republics, and Russia will determine America's role in the region. After decades of confrontation, the United States is deeply interested in establishing constructive relations with Russia. The development of these relations will depend on Russia's ability to change itself in three ways: to develop democracy, to form a market economy, and to evolve into a state that does not seek to dominate the peoples and nations around it. While the first two reforms are accepted by most Russian politicians, few accept the full independence of the "near abroad," although many renounce reassertion of centralized control.

This presents a dilemma for the United States. In its eagerness to support President Yeltsin's halting efforts to achieve political and economic transformation, the United States wishes to avoid confrontation with Russia over its failure to treat the republics as sovereign nations, especially since Moscow is now far more cooperative with the West on international issues in areas outside the former Soviet Union (such as the Middle East). Nor does Washington want to make President Yeltsin and his Foreign Ministry any more vulnerable to attack from Russian nationalists than they already are. On the other hand, the United States has recognized the other republics' independence and cannot condone Russian interventionism.

Critics have scored Washington for Russocentrism in handling the tricky question of Russia's stance on relations between the old "center" and the republics of the former Soviet Union.[5] They believe that sacrificing Central Asia's sovereignty for good relations with Russia and its cooperation on other issues is unwise and unfair. They argue that Washington may in fact be encouraging Russian aggression by fostering a sense of impunity for its actions toward its neighbors. Furthermore, opposing interventionism may further other U.S. policy aims in Russia, since a renunciation of special claims over the other republics (and the associated costs of making good on those claims) is arguably a precondition for Russia's successful transformation into a market democracy.

In fact, policymaking on Central Asia is not that simple. The contradictory nature of post-Soviet relations, with Central Asian republics highly dependent on Russia and formally joined to it under the amorphous CIS, complicates positions on heavy-handed Russian involvement in the region. Are Russian troops in Tajikistan peacekeepers acting under CIS mutual security agreements, or occupiers whose presence confirms the republic's status as a protectorate of Moscow? Is it even possible to separate the two roles? The Russian term for the troops in Tajikistan—*mirotvorcheskie sily* or, literally, "peacemaking forces"—perhaps most accurately reflects their stabilizing yet interventionist role in the country's affairs.

In any case, U.S. leverage in Central Asia is limited. American attention and resources are focused elsewhere. The U.S. presence is likely to increase as businesses move into the resource-rich region and begin to tap its markets. With the growth in economic relations, political interest in the republics will also rise. However, like every other country's for the foreseeable future, the U.S. government's position in Central Asia will be overshadowed by its relations with Moscow.

---

5. See, for instance, Zbigniew Brzezinski, "The Premature Partnership," *Foreign Affairs*, Vol. 73, no. 2 (March/April 1994).

Looking to the Future

Given that the modern republics of Central Asia have only begun to establish themselves as independent states, it is singularly difficult to predict how they will develop. Perhaps the only firm forecast one can make is that these countries are bound to change considerably as they continue to emerge from their Soviet pasts; as one Western observer commented, "Chances are that Central Asia today only dimly reflects the kind of Central Asia that we will see 50 years from now."[1] The Central Asian states' development will depend on how each addresses its three major challenges: the construction of a national identity, the establishment of economic viability, and the working out of relations with Russia and the Russians.

Culturally, the five republics will become less Russian and more focused on their dominant indigenous populations. The increase in indigenous birth rates over the past three decades and the emigration of Russians and other European populations ensure that Kazakhstan, the Kyrgyz Republic, and, to a lesser extent, the other republics, will have greater ethnic homogeneity. At the same time, Russia's cultural imprint will remain quite strong in at least the cities, since three of these peoples—the Kazakhs, Kyrgyz, and Turkmens—became urbanized and all of the peoples underwent industrialization with heavy Russian participation.

Political development in Central Asia is likely to be erratic. The concentration of power in the hands of the current leaders may provide stability for the present, but it also tends to stunt the

---

1. Graham E. Fuller, "Central Asia: The Quest for Identity," *Current History*, April 1994.

development of a body politic. Although Presidents Karimov, Nazarbaev, and Niyazov are firmly ensconced, they do not appear to be grooming successors. And while all three have promised to foster democracy, there are few examples of trouble-free transition from one-man rule to a system in which a variety of interests can compete without conflict. The Kyrgyz Republic's President Akaev has promoted pluralism, but the population, harried by economic problems, has shown little interest in the amateur parties that have arisen, and the Communist-era bureaucracy continues to be the only powerful political force in the country. Although the significance of clan divisions and the level of hardship vary among the republics, these factors will make smooth political transition even more difficult throughout Central Asia.

With the exception of Tajikistan, the republics have already moved far in taking control of their economies, although often less by design than by force of circumstances. There are signs that all of the Central Asian republics, except perhaps for gas-rich Turkmenistan, are prepared to go through with the reforms necessary to create viable national economies. Attempts to diversify cultivation, such as Turkmenistan's and Uzbekistan's reduction in cotton crops, and the development of industrial production to serve the needs of the local population better will continue, but slowly. At the same time, the process of economic reorientation will cause social dislocation, which may prompt significant popular backlash.

There will be increasingly large gaps among the economies of the Central Asian republics because of the uneven distribution of resources. On one end of the scale, Turkmenistan's gas and oil wealth combined with its small population should allow it to become a very rich nation in the near future. Kazakhstan also has a favorable ratio of natural resources to population in addition to possessing a stronger industrial and agricultural base. Uzbekistan too can rely on significant revenues from its metals, natural gas, and agriculture to fund development, although its resources-to-population ratio is not as good and it faces ethnic problems in the Fergana Valley. On the other end of the spectrum, the Kyrgyz Republic and Tajikistan are both relatively resource-poor and remote; they will have a far more difficult time in building national prosperity. Tajikistan's disadvantages are exacerbated by its civil

LOOKING TO THE FUTURE

war; as Tajikistani officials admit, the republic will be lucky if it is able to reach even pre-civil-war standards in the next three years.

Perceptions of fairness in the respective governments' distribution of wealth, particularly earnings from extractive industries which now go almost exclusively to state coffers, will become an increasingly important issue. After 70 years of official egalitarianism and the past few years of widespread want, governments will have to avoid creating large income gaps that could be seized upon by disenchanted ethnic or regional groupings. Discrepancies are already beginning to appear in Turkmenistan, even though President Niyazov has made several gestures to the population, such as making utilities free of charge. When the oil dollars start flowing into Kazakhstan in the next few years, the republic's government may face bitterness from ethnic groups (Kazakhs, Russians, or both) who feel that they are not receiving a fair share.

For the next few years, Russia will be in a position to control events in Central Asia. Over the decades, however, alternative roads, railroads, and especially pipelines through China, Iran, and Pakistan will give Central Asian countries more leverage in dealing with their dominant neighbor to the north. Of course, this will affect only those countries with significant export potential (which for Central Asia right now means the producers of raw materials such as hydrocarbons or metals), namely, Kazakhstan, Turkmenistan, and Uzbekistan. The Kyrgyz Republic and especially Tajikistan will continue to rely heavily on Russia.

The Central Asian countries are still fragile entities. If Vladimir Zhirinovsky or some other radical nationalist leader were to come to power in Moscow, Russia could conceivably move to bring the republics back under its control by force. The many divisions within the republics, not the least of which are the significant ethnic Russian minorities, might easily be exploited to undermine stability, which "peacemaking forces" from Russia could restore. However, Russia's ability to manipulate events will diminish with time as the Central Asian republics develop a sense of their own national identity, along with economies that serve their own needs rather than those of the old "center."

The experience of other colonial European populations suggests that the Russians will eventually leave the republics of Central Asia, except perhaps for those living in northern and eastern

Kazakhstan. However, there are important differences in the Russians' situation, which at the very least will stretch out the process of emigration for decades. First, the Russian emigrants face a less hospitable homeland than did the French in North Africa or the British in India. Russia is and will be much shorter of housing and funds, while the number of compatriots now located abroad is far greater, than was the case for other European powers. Significantly, there is already a small flow of Russians returning to their homes in Central Asia because life is too hard for them in Russia. Second, the Russians will be welcome as skilled labor for at least a generation, until members of the indigenous population can replace them.

Ties will grow with other countries, particularly an increasingly dynamic, powerful China. However, in the absence of extreme provocation from Moscow, the Central Asian republics are unlikely to form an anti-Russian bloc with other regional powers. The republics will move closer to Turkey, Iran, and Pakistan culturally and economically, but they are not going to come under any of these countries' dominant influence.

The Central Asian republics will have to reach agreements among themselves over the basic issues of sharing the region's limited water resources and infrastructure. In the long run, the countries will also probably complement one another economically to a greater extent. Although the differences within the region appear to preclude the formation of a political bloc, more populous and central Uzbekistan is likely to exert significant influence over its smaller neighbors to the south and east (as it already is doing in Tajikistan).

The republics of Central Asia came into being as fragments of a great empire that collapsed because it could no longer afford the costs or maintain the skills to manage itself. They remain disjointed fragments, still less well connected to one another than to their failed hub, operating for the most part under indigenous members of the same management team that brought the empire down. Their ability to coalesce will affect their survival as individual units.

The magnetism of Central Asia's natural wealth is attracting help and attention from other countries of the world. The future will depend on the extent to which these resources and management skills become available from the West, and the speed to which they can be put to use by local leaders under the watchful and suspicious eye of a Russia competing for the same kind of attention. Those republics that are able to balance these forces, and attain political and economic stability, will become hubs in their own right and create a new center of trade and investment at the heart of the Eurasian landmass.

A Note on Sources

Most of the information provided in this study is culled from numerous interviews with government officials, opposition figures, scholars, and both local and foreign journalists, as well as from literature produced in the United States, Russia, and the Central Asian republics themselves. The Asia Society thanks all those who gave their time and observations to the interviewers.

Figures for population are based on mid-1993 estimates provided by the Bureau of the Census, Center for International Research. Maps are adapted from versions provided by the Cartographic Section of the Department of Public Information at the United Nations.

Economic indicators are from the Statistics Committee of the Commonwealth of Independent States or official sources in the respective republics' governments. Given the often imprecise nature of calculation in the former USSR and the difficulties of gauging the major changes affecting the former socialist republics as they develop national market economies, figures on GDP, consumer price indices, and other key indicators do not reflect the state of these countries' economies to nearly the same degree as they do in more established market economies in the West. For instance, the 13 percent decrease in GDP for Kazakhstan in 1993 does not take into account much of the new kinds of production springing up in the republic's presently chaotic and largely unregulated economy (it is indicative that energy production fell by only 6 percent during the same period). In addition, some of the decline in GDP may well be healthy, reflecting a scaling-down of the production of goods for which there is little demand, a common problem in the former Soviet Union's military-oriented economy. Despite their shortcomings, these official figures are nonetheless the best available approximation of the fluid economic situation in Central Asia.

A Note on Names and Spellings

One of the first things the peoples of Central Asia did when they began to reclaim their cultural heritage during the waning years of the Soviet Union was to change Russified place names. This led to substantial confusion. For instance, the city of Frunze became Bishkek in 1991, while the name of the country of which it is the capital went from Kirgizia to Kyrgyzstan before finally becoming the Kyrgyz Republic in 1993. Both old and new names are used interchangeably in common parlance. In addition, many spellings were altered to reflect the rendering of names in the local native language; for example, Alma-Ata, the capital of Kazakhstan, became Almaty and Ashkhabad, Turkmenia, became Ashgabat, Turkmenistan. In particular, an "a" in Russian is commonly written as an "o" in the local languages. Names of persons are also affected, as some Central Asians have decided to drop the Russian "ov" or "ev" at the end of their surnames. The fact that indigenous languages use various modified forms of the Cyrillic alphabet adds to the confusion of rendering names in English.

We use the established English variants when possible. For instance, "Tajikistan" is used instead of the closest direct transliteration from the Tajik/Cyrillic, "Tochikiston." In cases where there is no common English rendering, we transliterate from the indigenous language.

Finally, we refer to the administrative subdivisions in each of the five republics as "oblasts," a Russian term that remains in common use in Central Asia (although most countries use a different name in the local language), which translates as "regions."

Written Sources in English

Books

Akhmedov, E. *Republic of Uzbekistan: A Reference Book.* Tashkent: Uzbekiston, 1993.

Karimov, I. A. *Uzbekistan: The Road of Independence and Progress.* Tashkent: Uzbekiston, 1992.

Mandelbaum, Michael, ed. *Central Asia and the World.* New York: Council on Foreign Relations Press, 1994.

Verkhovsky, Alexander. *Central Asia and Kazakhstan: A Political Spectrum.* Moscow: Panorama Publishing House, 1993.

World Bank. *Trends in Developing Economies: Extracts.* Vol. 1, *Eastern Europe and Central Asia.* Washington, D.C., 1993.

Articles and Reports

Amnesty International. "Amnesty International Report 1993" (1993).

Brown, Bess. "Central Asia: The Economic Crisis Deepens." *RFE/RL Report*, Vol. 3, no. 3 (January 7, 1994), pp. 59-69.

Brown, Bess. "Three Central Asian States Form Economic Union." *RFE/RL Report*, Vol. 3, no. 13 (April 1, 1994), pp. 33-35.

Brzezinski, Zbigniew. "The Premature Partnership." *Foreign Affairs*, Vol 73, no. 2 (March/April 1994).

"Central Asia." A compilation of articles in *Current History*, Vol. 93, no. 582 (April 1994).

Crow, Suzanne. "Russia Asserts Its Strategic Agenda." *RFE/RL Report*, Vol. 2, no. 50 (December 17, 1993), pp. 33-35.

Far Eastern Economic Review. "Central Asian Republics." *Asia 1994 Yearbook*, pp. 106-112.

Fuller, Graham E. "Central Asia: The Quest for Identity." *Current History* (April 1994).

Helsinki Watch/Human Rights Watch. "Human Rights in Tajikistan: In the Wake of Civil War" (December 1993).

Helsinki Watch/Human Rights Watch. "Human Rights in Turkmenistan" (May 1993).

Helsinki Watch/Human Rights Watch. "Human Rights in Uzbekistan" (May 1993).

Hill, Fiona, and Pamela Jewett. "'Back in the USSR': Russia's Intervention in the Internal Affairs of the Former Soviet Republics and the Implications for United States Policy Toward Russia." Report of the Strengthening Democratic Institutions Project, John F. Kennedy School of Government, Harvard University (January 1994).

Human Rights Watch. "Human Rights Watch World Report 1994" (December 1993).

Marnie, Sheila, and Erik Whitlock. "Central Asia and Economic Integration." *RFE/RL Report*, Vol. 2, no. 14 (April 2, 1993), pp. 34-44.

Martin, Keith. "Tajikistan: Civil War without End?" *RFE/RL Report*, Vol. 2, no. 33 (August 20, 1993), pp. 18-29.

Olcott, Martha Brill. "Central Asia's Catapult to Independence." *Foreign Affairs*, Vol. 7, no. 3 (Summer 1992), pp. 108-130.

Roy, Olivier. "The Civil War in Tajikistan: Causes and Implications." Report of the Study Group on the Prospects for Conflict and Opportunities for Peacemaking in the Southern Tier of Former Soviet Republics. Washington, D.C.: United States Institute of Peace, 1993.

Rubin, Barnett R. "The Fragmentation of Tajikistan." Draft article provided by the author.

Written Sources in Russian

Books

Gosudarstvennyi komitet SSSR po statistike (USSR State Statistics Committee). *Natsional'nyi sostav naseleniia SSSR* (Ethnic Composition of the USSR's Population). Moscow: Finansy i statistika, 1991.

Karimov, I.A. *O prioritetakh ekonomicheskoi politiki Uzbekistana* (On the Priorities of Uzbekistan's Economic Policy). Tashkent: Uzbekiston, 1993.

Kazakhstanskii institut strategicheskikh issledovanii (Kazakstan Institute of Strategic Studies). *Respublika Kazakhstan: Mezhetnicheskie aspekty sotsial'nykh i ekonomicheskikh reform* (Republic of Kazakstan: Interethnic Aspects of Social and Economic Reforms). Almaty: 1993.

Konstitutsiia Respubliki Uzbekistan (Constitution of the Republic of Uzbekistan). Tashkent: Uzbekiston, 1992.

Razakov, Talant. *Oshkie sobytie* (Osh Events). Bishkek: Renessans, 1993.

Statisticheskii komitet sodruzhestva nezavisimykh gosudarstv (Statistics Committee of the Commonwealth of Independent States). *Statisticheskii biulleten'* (Statistics Bulletin), Vol. 44, no. 2, January 1994.

Longer Articles and Reports

Briusina, O. I., and A. G. Osipov. "Mezhnatsional'nie otnosheniia: vsgliad na problemy Uzbekistana" (Interethnic Relations: A View of the Problems in Uzbekistan). *Vek XX: Etnichnost', obschestvo, gosudarstvo* (The Twentieth Century: Ethnicity, Society, and the State). Moscow: Russian Academy of Sciences, 1993.

Elebaeva, A. V., A. K. Jusupbekov, N. A. Omuraliev. "Oshkii mezhnatsional'nyi konflikt: sotsiologicheskii analiz" (Osh Interethnic Conflict: A Sociological Analysis). Bishkek: Academy of Sciences of Kyrgyzstan, 1991.

Kasenov, O. "Formula Evro-aziatskoi bezopasnosti" (A Formula of Eurasian Security). *Mysl* (Thought), no. 12 (1993).

Kasenov, O. "Ne rasdeliai i ne vlastvui: Tsentral'naia Azia i Rossiia vmeste ili porozn'?" (Do Not Divide and Do Not Rule: Central Asia and Russia Together or Apart?). *Poisk* (Search), no. 49 (December 10-16, 1993).

Kasenov, O. "Okazhet'sia li Tsentral'naia Aziia v vodovorote geopoliticheskikh igr? Razmyshleniia po povodu predlozhenii rossiiskikh analitikov" (Will Central Asia End Up in a Whirlpool of Geopolitical Games? Thoughts on Russian Analysts' Suggestions). *Aziia* (Asia), no. 1 (1994).

Migranian, A. "Rossiya i blizhnie zarubezhie." *Nezavisimaya Gazeta*, January 5, 1994.

"Osnovnie Polozheniia voennoi doktriny Rossiiskoi Federatsii" (Fundamental Provisions of the Russian Federation's Military Doctrine). *Krasnaia zvezda* (Red Star), November 19, 1993.

"Rezul'taty raboty deputatskoi komissii Zhogorku Kenesha Kyrgyzskoi Respubliki po zolotu" (Results of the Work of the Deputies' Commission on Gold of the Jogorku Kenesh of the Kyrgyz Republic). (Bishkek: October 1993).

Shishkov, Iu., A. Elianov, N. Amrekulov. "Rossiia i tsentral'noaziatskie respubliki: problemy i perspektivy" (Russia and the Central Asian Republics: Problems and Prospects). *Mirovaia ekonomika i mezhdunarodnie otnoshenie* (World Economics and International Relations), no. 11 (three articles) (1993).

Study Mission Agenda

Nicholas Platt and Charles Undeland
January 16–29, 1994

January 16, Moscow, Russia

Meeting
Ambassador Thomas Pickering

January 17, Moscow

Meetings
1. Gennady Chufrin, Deputy Director, Institute of Oriental Studies, and Irina Zviagelskaia, Vice President, Russian Center of Strategic Research and International Studies
2. Abdunabi Satarzoda, Deputy Chairman of the Democratic Party of Tajikistan; Muhamed Dust, member of the Executive Council of the Democratic Party of Tajikistan; Gavar Juraeva, member of board, Tajik refugee organization *Umed* (Hope)
3. Abdurashid Sharipov, Deputy Director of the Moscow Center for Human Rights
4. Andrannik Migranian, member of the Presidential Council, Russian Federation
5. Bakhtier Khakimov, Head of South Asia and the Middle East Department, Foreign Ministry of the Russian Federation

January 18, Dushanbe, Tajikistan

Arrival in Dushanbe
Meetings
1. Rashid Olimov, Minister of Foreign Affairs
2. Shukurjon Zukhorov, Minister of Labor and Employment

3. General Yevgeny Bessmertnykh, Deputy Commander of the Joint Forces of the Commonwealth of Independent States in Tajikistan, and Captain Ivan Malevich, Press Secretary for the Joint Forces of the Commonwealth of Independent States in Tajikistan
4. Sanfin Hafeezov, Deputy Minister of Culture

January 19, Dushanbe

Meetings
1. Kozidavlat Koimdodov, Deputy Chairman of the Supreme Soviet
2. Liviu Bouta, Head of the United Nations Mission of Observers in Tajikistan
3. Makhmadamin Oimakhmadov, First Deputy Minister of Foreign Economic Relations
4. Stanley Escudero, Ambassador of the United States to Tajikistan

January 20

Travel from Dushanbe to Samarkand

January 21, Samarkand, Uzbekistan

Meetings
1. Nematjan Sadikov, representative of the Aga Khan Foundation in Samarkand
2. Gaibullo Ashurov, Head of Cultural Department, Samarkand Oblast Government
3. Nugman U. Makhmudov, Director of the National Museum of the People of Uzbekistan

January 22

Travel to Bukhara, Uzbekistan
Day in Bukhara
Return to Samarkand

THE CENTRAL ASIAN REPUBLICS

January 23

Day in Samarkand
Travel from Samarkand to Tashkent, Uzbekistan

January 24, Tashkent, Uzbekistan

Meetings
1. Naim Gaibov, Chairperson of the National Association for International Cultural and Humanitarian Relations of the Republic of Uzbekistan (NAMS); Shakhlo Makhmudova, Deputy Chairperson of NAMS; and Nadezhda Koblova, Head of U.S. and Europe Section of NAMS
2. Ulugbek Ishankhojaev, Head of U.S. Department, Ministry of Foreign Affairs
3. Djura A. Abdullaev, Minister of Higher and Secondary Education; Vyacheslav Golyshev, Acting Director of the Institute of World Problems of the Office of the President of the Republic of Uzbekistan; Khairuddin Masudov, Deputy Minister of Education; and Sabirjan Saidov, Senior Expert on Intergovernmental and Interethnic Relations of the Office of the President of the Republic of Uzbekistan
4. Henry Clarke, Ambassador of the United States to Uzbekistan

January 25, Tashkent

Meetings
1. Tokhtasin Gofourbekov, Director of the Institute of Art Research
2. Firowz Ashrafi, Chairman of the Union of Architects

Travel from Tashkent to Almaty, Kazakhstan

January 26, Almaty, Kazakhstan

Meetings
1. Oumerseric Kasenov, Director of the Kazakhstan Institute for Strategic Studies under the President of the Republic of Kazakhstan

2. William Courtney, Ambassador of the United States to Kazakhstan, and U.S. Embassy staff
3. Nursultan Nazarbaev, President of Kazakhstan; also present were Kassymjomart Tokaev, First Deputy Minister of Foreign Affairs, and Bulat Baektenov, Deputy Chairman of the Security Council
4. Oumerseric Kasenov and Erlan Arynov, Deputy Director of the Kazakhstan Institute for Strategic Studies under the President of the Republic of Kazakhstan

January 27, Almaty

Meetings
1. Serik Ashlaev, Minister of Culture, and Yevgeny Kotovoi, Deputy Minister of Culture
2. Serik Akhanov, Deputy Minister of Economics

Travel from Almaty to Bishkek, the Kyrgyz Republic

January 28, Bishkek, the Kyrgyz Republic

Meetings
1. Turar Koichuev, President of the National Academy of Sciences; Vladimir Ploskikh, Vice President of the National Academy of Sciences; Anatoly Frolin, Research Secretary of the National Academy of Sciences; and Esengul Beishembiev, Director of the Institute of State and Law
2. Alikbek Jekshenkulov, Deputy Minister of Foreign Affairs
3. Cholponbek Bazarbaev, Minister of Culture
4. Karim Urazbaev, First Deputy Minister of Economy and Finance
5. Chinara Jakypova, Director of the Center for Strategic Research and President, Scientific-Democratic Alliance
6. Edward Hurwitz, Ambassador of the United States to the Kyrgyz Republic

January 29

Travel from Bishkek to Almaty
Departure from Almaty

Additional Sources

Interviewed by Charles Undeland

In Moscow, Russia

Valentin Bushkov, senior researcher, and Olga Briusova and Igor Savin, researchers, Institute of Ethnography, Academy of Sciences of the Russian Federation

Muhamed Dust, member of the Executive Council of the Democratic Party of Tajikistan

Gavar Juraeva, member of board, Tajik refugee organization *Umed* (Hope) and member of board, Coordinating Center of Democratic Forces of Tajikistan

Tair Khalimov, Second Secretary, Embassy of Tajikistan

Abdy Kuliev, former Foreign Minister of Turkmenistan

Otakhon Latifi, Chairman of the Coordinating Council of Democratic Forces of Tajikistan

Madamanin Narzikulov, Director of the Society for the Furthering of the Observance of Human Rights in Central Asia and member of the Presidium of the Central Council of the *Birlik* movement

Vitaly Naumkin, Director, and Mavlon Makhkamov, researcher, Russian Center of Strategic Research and International Studies

Oleg Panfilov, journalist at *Nezavisimaya Gazeta*

Vitaly Ponamarev, analyst, Panorama Group

Bakhtier Urdashev and Shamkat Khamrakulov, Second Secretaries, Embassy of Uzbekistan

Alexander Petrov and Rachel Denver, Helsinki Watch/Human Rights Watch

In Ashgabat, Turkmenistan

Mukhametkerim Agaev, Deputy Head of the Department of Science and Education of the Cabinet of Ministers

Batir Berdiev, Deputy Minister of Foreign Affairs, and Mukhamet Jutdiev, Head of Information, Department of Ministry of Foreign Affairs

Lyalya Nazarova, Department on Foreign Economic Relations, Economics Institute of the Cabinet of Ministers

Ron Trigg, Political Officer of the Embassy of the United States

In Almaty, Kazakhstan

Apsimet Arganbaev, Center for Sociology and Interethnic Relations

Emin Bilgic, Counsellor for Economic Relations, Embassy of Turkey

Leslie Davidson, Second Secretary, Embassy of the United States

Rustem Janguzhin, publicist and Doctor of Philosophy, Academy of Sciences

Oumerseric Kasenov, Director of the Kazakhstan Institute for Strategic Studies under the President of the Republic of Kazakhstan

Khalid Khattak, Commercial Secretary, Embassy of Pakistan

Seidakhmet Kuttykadamov, Deputy Minister of Press and Information

Erkesh Nurpeisov, Director, Institute of State and Law

John Richotte, Central Asian representative for the National Democratic Institute of the U.S. Democratic Party

Marat Tazhin, Director, Institute of Analytical Studies of the Office of the President

Vitaly Voronov, former Deputy Chairman of the Supreme Soviet Committee on Human Rights, and Alexander Peregrin, member of the Supreme Soviet Committee on Human Rights

Sabit Zhusupov, Director, Republican Center for Public Opinion and Market Research

In Bishkek, the Kyrgyz Republic

Kamel Bailinov, correspondent for *Komsomol'skaya Pravda*

Lisa Batey, representative for the Central and East European Law Initiative Project of the American Bar Association

Ainura Elebaeva, Doctor of Philosophy, Academy of Sciences

Yevgeny Kablukov and Akylbek Saleev, experts in the International Department of the Office of the President of the Kyrgyz Republic

Emilbek Kaptagaev, Head of Department of Socio-Political Analysis and Prognosis of the Government of the Kyrgyz Republic

Chinara Jakypova, Director of the Center for Strategic Research and President, Scientific-Democratic Alliance

Bermet Malikova, correspondent for *Interfax*

Erkin Mamkulov, Head of Section on Central Asia and the Trans-Caucasus, Ministry of Foreign Affairs

Harry Trines, resident representative of the International Monetary Fund

Benjamin Tua, Deputy Chief of Mission, Embassy of the United States

In Osh, the Kyrgyz Republic

Bakyt Beshimov, Rector, Osh University

In Dushanbe, Tajikistan

Rakhmangol Ataev, Chairman, Committee on International and Interethnic Relations of the Supreme Soviet

Liviu Bouta, Head of United Nations Mission of Observers in Tajikistan

Alexander Chubarov, Deputy Minister of Defense

Stanley Escudero, Ambassador of the United States to Tajikistan

Kurban Sattorov, Chairman, Uzbek Society

Antoine Koechlin, Head of Delegation, International Committee of the Red Cross

Michel Svantner, Field Officer, Office of the United Nations High Commissioner for Refugees

Valery Yushin, Chairman, Russian Society

In Tashkent, Uzbekistan

Darya Fein, Political Officer, Embassy of the United States

Vyacheslav Golyshev, Acting Director of the Institute of World Problems of the Office of the President of the Republic of Uzbekistan

Alisher Ikramov, Head of International Department, University of World Economics and Diplomacy

Alan Johnston, British Broadcasting Corporation correspondent

Sabirjan Saidov, Senior Expert on Intergovernmental and Interethnic Affairs of the Office of the President of the Republic of Uzbekistan

About the Authors

Charles Undeland began working in the former Soviet Union in 1990 as a translator for the Russian weekly *Literaturnaya gazeta* and as a desk assistant at the Moscow bureau of ABC News. In the summer of 1991 he translated for a UNESCO-sponsored expedition retracing the Silk Road through then-Soviet Central Asia. After receiving his B.A. from Brown University in 1992, Mr. Undeland returned to Moscow as a research assistant for Harvard University's Strengthening Democratic Institutions Project. He worked full-time as a consultant on Central Asia for The Asia Society from October 1993 to May 1994. He is now a program officer for Central Asia at the National Endowment for Democracy.

Nicholas Platt became the fifth president of The Asia Society in November 1992, after serving as U.S. Ambassador to the Islamic Republic of Pakistan. He has also held ambassadorial posts in the Philippines (1987-91) and Zambia (1982-84).

Ambassador Platt's involvement with Asia began early in his foreign service career when he studied the Chinese language in Taiwan. He was a political officer in Hong Kong (1964-68), Beijing (1973-74), and Tokyo (1974-77). After 1977 Ambassador Platt served in several capacities in Washington, including China analyst, Director of Japanese Affairs, National Security Staff Member for Asian Affairs, Deputy Assistant Secretary of Defense (responsible for political and military relations with Japan, Korea, China, and Southeast Asia), Acting Assistant Secretary of State for U.N. Affairs (1981-82), and Executive Secretary of the Department of State (1985-87).

Ambassador Platt graduated from Harvard College and received an M.A. degree from the Johns Hopkins University School of Advanced International Studies. He is a member of the New York Council on Foreign Relations and the International Institute for Strategic Studies, London.